The Winter Camping Handbook

Wilderness Travel & Adventure in the Cold-Weather Months

Stephen Gorman

The Countryman Press
Woodstock, Vermont

We welcome your comments and suggestions. Please contact Editor, The Countryman Press, P.O. Box 748, Woodstock, Vermont 05091, or e-mail countrymanpress@wwnorton.com.

Copyright © 2007 by Stephen Gorman

Portions of this book were previously published under the title *Winter Camping* by the Appalachian Mountain Club.

ISBN 978-0-88150-782-9

Book design and composition by Faith Hague Book Design
Cover photo © PatitucciPhoto/Aurora Photos
Interior photos by the author unless otherwise specified
Map on page 189 by Mapping Specialists Ltd., Madison, WI,
   © The Countryman Press

Published by The Countryman Press, P.O. Box 748, Woodstock, VT 05091

Distributed by W. W. Norton & Company, Inc., 500 Fifth Avenue, New York, NY 10110

Printed in the United States of America

10 9 8 7 6 5 4 3 2 1

Contents

Preface

How things change. The other day I was rereading sections of the first edition of this book, published back in 1991, and I realized just how far we winter-sports enthusiasts have come in the intervening years.

Think back a moment to those Dark Ages, a misty, distant time before plastic telemark boots; before wide, shaped skis; before split snowboards. I got a good chuckle when I read my description of the ideal backcountry ski as "double-cambered and having measurements of 65-55-60 mm." And they were probably 210 centimeters long to boot.

Yikes! Who could ski on such long, skinny sticks? My current single-camber skis are essentially twice that fat and 35 centimeters shorter. (Back then I also mentioned that a good pair of skis would cost you "somewhere between $200 and $300." Ah well, you can double that too.)

And how about ski boots? Good grief! Back in the early 1990s, according to that classic first edition, good backcountry boots were "sturdy, torsionally rigid leather hiking boots with an extended sole for clipping into the binding toe piece." I then described the newfangled Merrell Super Comp (for those of you too young to know, it was a boot combining a plastic upper and a leather, lace-up lower) as "too heavy and too stiff for anything but lift-served skiing."

Imagine. Today, my plastic telemark ski boots are virtually indistinguishable from those worn by Alpine ski racers. My, my.

These days I look back and wonder how I ever made turns with that flimsy leather boot–skinny ski setup. No wonder I spent so much time digging myself out of the snowpack!

And think about this: In those days the notion of a snowboarder accessing the backcountry was basically ludicrous. In fact, we hardly knew what a snowboard was back then!

I went through that first edition, and I found references to all sorts of funny anachronisms: three-pin bindings, avalanche cords, you name it. Though much of the information it contained remains timeless, I realized that the good old book was in need of a major overhaul.

So here it is, a new and improved, updated edition for a new era of adventures in snow. It's chock full of new information, new images, and entirely new sections to help you navigate the winter wilds in comfort and safety. Hope you enjoy it, and have fun out there!

Introduction

I awoke in the dark to the sound of wind rushing through the pass. The tent shook and the fly snapped—but as I lay still in my sleeping bag, I could hear something else: the whisper of falling snowflakes brushing the fabric of the tent.

Quietly, I pulled on my boots and parka, taking care not to wake my companions, and stepped into the swirling storm. The snow was coming down hard. It filled the snowshoe tracks from the night before and wiped away all trace of last night's fire. As the birches and balsams shook and the snow whipped the air, I enjoyed a peaceful, almost euphoric, moment until I could stand it no longer: "HEY YOU GUYS, WAKE UP! IT'S SNOWING!"

Just for good measure, I pelted the tent with snowballs and then dashed to the trees for kindling and firewood.

This is winter camping: the splendid forest scenery, the grace of falling snow, and the companionship of friends. These have a way of making you feel like a kid again. Who doesn't have cherished memories of being snowed in—the unexpected gift of a day away from work or school? Who isn't gripped by a sense of adventure when snow forces a change of plan?

Winter camping is like being snowed in. It makes us free from sched-

Golf carts buried in snow: I guess it's time to hang up the clubs and grab the skis!

Winter camping may mean free heeling into the outback, as a telemarker does here in the Chic-Choc Mountains on the Gaspé Peninsula in Quebec.

ules and demands. It offers an opportunity to be self-reliant, to feel the deep satisfaction of a snug shelter or a warm fire. It gives us the chance to slow down, renew old friendships, and enjoy life again.

And winter camping provides a chance to play—to slide down a steep slope on your skis and land in a snowy pile at the bottom, to dig snow caves and to build igloos, to bombard your friends with snowballs, to have fun.

And fun is what winter camping is really all about. As the Indians and Eskimos of the far north demonstrate, life in the cold need not be all hardship and danger. Winter can be the favorite season, the time when frozen lakes, rivers, and snow-filled forests make perfect highways for fast and easy travel. It's the time when animals can be located more easily; it's the bug-free season when the land seems strangely empty and silent.

It's also the time when the snow provides a slippery surface to send skis and sleds swiftly on their way, when the land is magically transformed from the drab grays and browns of late fall to sparkling blues and crisp whites.

Living indoor lives, shielded from the elements by our computer-age technology, warmed by fossil fuels and nuclear power, many of us now see winter as the enemy, something to be survived. We shake our heads in wonder at people who spend time outdoors in the cold and snow. We've forgotten the pleasures of winter outings.

This book is dedicated to helping you discover the pleasures of snow camping and deals mostly with the fundamentals. It is designed to take you through the steps of planning, organizing, and conducting a trip on your own. As an introductory volume, the book is written for those who wish to explore the winter wilderness and experience the joys of winter travel in warmth, comfort, and safety.

Chapter 1

Wintering

H idden under the snowy forest canopy, locked beneath the ice of freshwater lakes and tucked away in the hollows of fallen trees, life in winter continues. Though the land looks still, the residents are going about their business. After all, here in the north, winter lasts half the year or more. Natural processes can't afford to hang fire for six or eight months. There's too much to do.

All life in cold environments prepares carefully for the onset of winter. Essentially, animals use one of three strategies for wintering: migration, hibernation, and adaptation. Animals that migrate survive winter by fleeing to warmer climates. By escaping winter, they avoid its rigors altogether, but they pay a hefty price in terms of energy consumed, and success isn't guaranteed. Precious energy reserves may be depleted before the animal reaches its hoped-for destination.

Though migration as a wintering strategy appeals to many people, and mass human migrations occur every fall and spring, the cost is too high for most, and migration simply is not an option for everyone.

Some animals find a snug shelter, enter a state of reduced activity while maintaining their body temperatures above freezing, and hibernate. Yet because the animal must find a den where the temperature doesn't drop much below freezing, and the chance of finding such a safe haven diminishes the farther north it goes, hibernation as a strategy is rare among northern animals.

Hibernation is not a strategic option for people, though many endure a self-imposed imprisonment during the cold season, growing daily more lethargic and suffering from a malady called cabin fever.

Since avoiding winter through migration and hibernation just doesn't work for most northern animals, people included, the alternative is to adapt. Adapting means staying active and alert and coping with the seasonal changes in the physical environment. Wolves and caribou, fox and snow-shoe hare act out their ancient relationships through the long Arctic winter. And people, too, adapt to life in the north, wintering successfully when they adjust to the season rather than fight it. Those who refuse, who instead try to impose an artificial lifestyle of perpetual summer upon the winter environment, face chronic discontent when the snow flies and the temperature drops.

The Athabaskan and Algonquian Indians of North America's interior forests and the Eskimos of the Arctic regions perfected winter living and travel techniques over ten thousand years. For them, the winter environment is home. They've devised clothing, shelter, and methods of travel most appropriate for the cold months. Northern peoples have always found an ally in winter. The season makes their lives easier, not harder. Northern Natives depend upon winter; they don't exist despite it. Winter makes life in the north possible and is the determining factor in how people live and travel.

Adapting to a winter environment requires the proper clothing and skill.

For the hunter, mobility is of paramount importance. The ability to cover vast areas in search of elusive and widely dispersed game animals is critical to survival. Snow provides that mobility. Cold, hard, wind-packed snow is a surface that enables hunters in the barrens to cover a hundred or more miles per day by dog team. Snowmobiles, of course, need snow to cover equal if not greater distances.

In the interior forests, the frozen surfaces of an endless maze of lakes and rivers serve as a natural highway. Deep snow in the forest buries thick tangles of brush,

Ski tracks lead to a protected tent campsite in Wyoming's Grand Tetons.

which hamper travel in summer. Speed and ease of travel is greatly enhanced by the onset of cold weather, and this increased efficiency is crucial to those who provide for themselves.

Europeans, particularly the French, were quick to adopt Native technologies for their winter travel in the North American wilderness. French fur trappers and traders recognized the importance of living among the native peoples: Earning their trust and learning their ways was the best method of doing business. Among the French, to be a *voyageur*, a member of the great fur-trading brigades that traveled "up country" among the Indians, was to be among the elite. To be an *hivernant,* one who spent the winter in the field, was to have earned the highest distinction of all.

Today, it's perhaps harder than ever for outsiders to understand these relationships to the changing seasons. As we rely less on our own skills and less on predictable seasonal patterns, and as we alter our environment to serve us, direct contact with our surroundings becomes seemingly less important or beneficial. Modern culture insists you can't be comfortable when removed from the amenities of the latest technology, that living outdoors means "roughing it"—and who needs it rough? Not

Whether on snowshoes, a snowboard, telemark skis, or alpine touring skis, there are many ways to access the winter wilds.

George W. Sears, a self-described "old woodsman" who, in the 1920s, wrote under the pseudonym Nessmuk.

On the subject of "roughing it," Nessmuk writes: "I dislike the phrase. We do not go to [the woods] to rough it. We go to smooth it. We get it rough enough at home; in towns and cities; in shops, offices, stores, banks. . . . [D]on't rough it; make it as smooth, as restful and pleasurable as you can."

The best way to smooth out the rough spots, to be assured of a safe and comfortable winter experience, is to develop a sound set of skills. Skills give you the edge in your wilderness travels. With well-developed skills, you can move through the country efficiently and with little impact, taking advantage of what your surroundings have to offer. You learn to avoid hazards and to develop the confidence to handle critical situations. There is simply no substitute for skill.

Anthropologists, ethnographers, Native elders, and others decry the fact that modern industrial society and its technology are rapidly replacing the traditional skills of indigenous peoples. They worry that healthy, viable cultures are being obliterated, that soon, traditional methods and ways of life and the relationships to the earth that they imply will be lost forever. And indigenous peoples are not the only ones whose skills are vanishing, whose relationships with the natural world are suffering.

Yet there are still those, Native and non-Native alike, who are expert in the skills of wilderness living. Being an expert need not be a function of your job or even of how much time you spend in the field. A person can make the same mistakes year after year—I know people who do. As writer and outdoorsman Cliff Jacobson says, "Experts are distinguished by the style in which they travel, not by the difficulty of the trip, the frequency of those trips, or the number of days out." Style and skill are synonymous.

Snow School

Why was there so much more snow when we were younger?

It's not necessarily global warming that produces what seems like less snow now. Indeed, there are many nonclimatic reasons for this common perception, such as the fact that you were shorter when you were young, and snow banks looked much higher. Another reason is that snow removal practices have improved dramatically in the last few decades. Finally, we all tend to remember extreme events and think of them as representing the norm. •

A high skill level is the result of patience, understanding, and respect—the essential energies put into a carefully nurtured relationship. By paying attention, by not imposing, we can hear what the land is saying. The dry snap of a twig teaches about kindling. The hollow sound of thin ice warns of danger. Wind informs us of a coming storm. The calm silence of a snow cave speaks of sanctuary when the furies howl outside.

Returning to winter, even for a few days, allows us to renew our relationship with the land and with ourselves. By listening, by paying attention, we can rediscover the fulfillment of coming home again and understand what Quebec poet Gilles Vigneault means when he says, "My country is not a country, it is the winter."

Chapter 2

Planning

Experiencing the unexpected—a great view or campsite, a foot of new powder on the downhill run—is one of the best parts of backcountry travel. If you plan well, you'll probably enjoy several of these unforeseen pleasures on your trip. But if you're casual about planning and shortcut the process, you're far more likely to experience an unexpected disappointment, as happened to me not too long ago.

The snowy surface of New Hampshire's Lake Umbagog stretched like a white tabletop toward Canada. Under a gorgeous blue sky, our two dog sleds moved briskly over the smooth surface. We were making great time, conditions were right; everything was going according to plan.

We turned the dogs to the east, planning to intersect a trail marked clearly on our topographic maps. The trail, shown as a series of dashes coursing through an unbroken area of green, went overland through the trees.

But there were no trees. We climbed a steep hill, passed through a veneer of conifers, and emerged on a desolate wasteland stretching as far as we could see. Here, where the map indicated forest, was a massive clearcut—industrial blight on an enormous scale. The early stages of planning can make or break your trip. We had put our faith in the maps and paid the price. Gathering as much information as possible before you set out is critical to the success of your trip.

Where to Go

One of the big differences between winter and summer camping is that in winter the backcountry expands. The crowds of summer are gone, and the carrying capacity of the landscape is no longer stretched beyond a sensible level. A popular summer hiking area reverts to a near wilderness when the snow falls. In winter, a rare encounter with another group of campers is not an intrusion, as it is in summer, but a welcome chance to share a moment with new friends. It's as if the winter wilderness is larger, more remote, more pristine. Wherever you go, close to home or far away, you're bound to discover new delights.

The first step is to decide on an area. Using guidebooks, the Internet, road maps, or an atlas, you can pick an area of the country—or the world— that you want to visit. Now is the time to think big if you want a true wilderness adventure or think small if you want a more personal, intimate experience. Get yourself psyched up. Cut out pictures and maps of the area and tape them to the refrigerator. Talk about it with your friends or whoever will listen. Read the accounts of those who have been there. Project yourself into the landscape; savor the daydreams on your way to work.

There may be great winter camping right outside your doorstep. You can save time, gas, and money by not traveling long distances. A favorite local hiking area can be a great place for winter camping. Becoming familiar with a small wilderness may be as satisfying to you as trekking across a vast, expansive tract. Think about what you want your winter camping to be: Do you want to take an easy, relaxing trip, or do you want to challenge yourself and push your limits? You may want to mix it up a bit, blending relaxation and challenge into your own personal recipe for adventure.

Next, while you're still riding the crest of enthusiasm, gather more information. Make a list of people to contact: state, provincial, and federal

Winter camping can mean traveling to remote areas and seeing unusual sights, such as this inukshuk, or "stone man," guarding the entrance to a pass in far northern Quebec.

land management agencies; local hiking clubs; specialty shop owners and employees. Talk with these people and pump them for information. When you've pumped them dry, ask where you can find out more. Write or e-mail people who have traveled where you're going. Ask them about routes, local conditions, the best time of year to go, and other pertinent information.

Simultaneously, start acquiring maps of the area. All maps—road maps, government maps, even tourist maps—contain useful information. And don't overlook maps put out by small publishing houses or local companies. These may not be as accurate as government topographic maps, but they may contain up-to-date information missing from official maps, especially where changes in land use have occurred.

Once you've gathered as much information as you can, make a base map. Take the topographic maps and draw in all the new information that you've rounded up from other sources. Draw in new logging roads, buildings, or other land-use changes. Note all the hazards or special sights people have told you about.

Pencil in your route, and check off every mile. Mark elevation gains and losses, and remember that climbing almost always takes longer in winter than in summer, whereas descending may be quicker. Note any physical features, such as open water, blown-down timber, or other obstacles that might cause delay. Try to find out what kind of weather and snow conditions you can reasonably expect. Then determine the distance you plan to cover each day of travel. Finally, look at your route and mark sheltered areas you can resort to in case of bad weather or injury. For each day of your trip, decide upon the quickest and safest way out in the event of an emergency, and mark these escape routes on your base map.

How Far?

How far should you plan to travel? That depends on a number of factors, such as the steepness or ruggedness of the terrain, the weight of your pack, your means of travel, the pace of your slowest companion, the amount of time you can allot for your trip, and the time of year.

If the snow is either slush or deep powder, expect tough going. If the snow has settled or the surface is firm and wind-packed, traveling will be much faster. In the mountains, covering 5 miles may make for an exhausting day. In a valley, on a plateau, or skiing across a lake or river, you may be able to cover 5 miles in a couple of hours.

Check the topographical map. If the contour lines are close together—

Be sure to plan for great views when you think about where to go and how far to travel.

indicating steep or rugged terrain—plan about 5 to 10 miles per day. If the going is flat and wind-packed, you may be able to knock off 10 to 15 miles or more per day.

There are no simple rules of thumb concerning distance you can cover. When in doubt, estimate conservatively. If you exceed your expectations, you can always take interesting side tours or enjoy a layover day. Some groups take a short trip into the wilderness to set up a base camp, then go on exciting day tours that are well within the group's capabilities.

When to Go

Late winter is an ideal time for your first trip or for a mountain trip. In temperate latitudes, the temperatures have moderated by late February or early March, the days are longer, and the accumulated snows of winter are piled high.

Also, at that time of year, animals respond to the increased light and warmth. Your chances of seeing signs of wildlife activity are probably better. Give yourself a chance to hone your skills in a more benign environment before tackling a midseason trip with more extreme conditions. Just remember that the longer you wait, the greater the likelihood that you'll run into rain and melting snow.

As you gain experience, you may time your trips to coincide with the cold periods, especially if you travel in areas where wide temperature fluctuations are common. Experienced travelers often consider cold an ally. Early or late-season lake and river ice can be dangerous, but hard, midwinter ice is a fabulous travel surface. Subzero temperatures without strong winds can actually be pleasant for traveling. In strong cold, you're less likely to sweat on the trail, easily maintaining a constant temperature while wearing only a few layers. Also, ice and snow conditions are good in cold periods, and rain is extremely unlikely.

Planning for Contingencies

Be flexible and realize that no matter how well you plan, nature can make a mockery of your best efforts. I once led an Outward Bound group that was determined to stick to its original itinerary, despite the fact that we were traversing a rugged mountain range that had received 13 inches of snow on the second day of the trip.

By the fifth day the group was totally exhausted, having slogged only 9 or 10 miles in three days. On the evening of the fifth day, the members of the group were frustrated and angry. They realized they would never reach their destination, and they certainly weren't having any fun. When my assistant and I suggested we consider getting off the ridge and descending to the gentle trails of the valley floor, they were stunned. Taking an alternative route had not occurred to them.

The next day, relieved of their burdensome goal, plunging down slopes through knee-deep drifts and skidding on their snowshoe tails, they had the time of their lives. The whole atmosphere of the trip changed.

Despite the best planning efforts, what's actually achievable depends upon local conditions at the time of your trip. Severe weather can move in and slow you down. Have a contingency plan prepared in advance. On your base map, note all the sheltered areas where you can find protection in case of a storm, and mark all the bail-out points along your route. Knowing your alternatives in advance will allow you to change your plan or retreat before you get into trouble. In the event of an emergency along the route, you'll already know the quickest way to help.

Permits and Restrictions

Note the various land jurisdictions your route crosses. National and state lands operate under different sets of regulations, and each may have a

As good as it gets: great views and perfect Alaskan spring corn

different mandate for use. A trip in the greater Yellowstone area, for example, may cross a patchwork of federal, state, municipal, private, and Indian lands. A trip in northern New England offers similar planning challenges, except that there the land is largely the property of timber corporations. A call to the government or the company woodlands manager will provide you with critical information.

Find out if there are any restrictions on winter travel in a specific area. Some parks, such as Maine's Baxter State Park, require that you apply in advance before you're admitted to the park in winter. If you learn about restrictions ahead of time, you won't be surprised.

When you've arrived at your destination, check in with any local authorities—National Park Service or Parks Canada rangers, state or provincial department of natural resources officials, Forest Service personnel, and others who are in charge of local land and resource management. You can find them in the local phone book.

Also, it's not a bad idea to talk to people in town for up-to-the-minute tips on the area. Outfitters, guides, and specialty-shop personnel are excellent sources of local knowledge. If you can, build in a day for gathering details concerning snow and ice conditions, weather forecasts, and trail information.

Spontaneity

John Muir apparently set out on his journeys with only the barest essentials and having done only minimal planning. For him, spontaneity was a virtue. H. W. Tillman, the great British mountaineer, once remarked that if he couldn't plan a Himalayan expedition on the back of an envelope, it wasn't worth doing. The joys of unanticipated discovery are great, but use your judgment.

Those who choose this type of adventure and survive have an incredible base of knowledge and skill. For them, heading off into the unknown is a shrewdly calculated risk, not a gamble. Yet it's usually wiser and safer to have as much information as possible before setting out.

Snow School

What was the greatest seven-day snowfall ever recorded in the United States?

At Thompson Pass, Alaska, 186.9 inches fell during the week ending February 25, 1953. •

Winterlude: The Right Stuff in Cold Places

When learning, remember to move at your own pace. Expand your zone of comfort, but don't step out of it. A solid base of skills will stand you in good stead. If a trip is too ambitious for you now, don't worry; if you stick to it, you'll be ready someday. The important thing is to have the right attitude. The experiences of two explorers illustrate the point.

The first, Sir John Franklin, was a likeable gentleman explorer commissioned by the British Admiralty in 1845 to discover the Northwest Passage through the Canadian Arctic. He was also a member of that school of imperial officers who were steadfast in their contempt for the environment and for Eskimo travel techniques. They clung to their notions of proper conduct, preferring to carry silver place settings and crystal decanters instead of more appropriate food and supplies. As they stumbled through the frozen landscape and slowly starved to death, the last survivors resorting to cannibalism before they too expired.

Roughing it indeed!

John Rae was a contemporary of Franklin but was a different breed. A tireless traveler in the service of the Hudson's Bay Company, he would journey more than 1,000 miles over the course of a winter, often covering more than 25 miles per day on snowshoes in one of the harshest climates on earth. Rae had no qualms about adopting Native techniques. He made a study of Eskimo skills, his "heretical notion," as one historian puts it, being "that northern travelers should harness the . . . environment to their advantage instead of struggling against it."

Predictably, the Admiralty disagreed with Rae, suggesting "The objective of . . . explorations is to explore properly and not to evade the hazards of the game through the vulgar subterfuge of going native." It was better to rough it as emissaries of a magnificent civilization than to smooth passage through the adaptation of indigenous methods.

Ironically, it was John Rae, certainly one of the greatest winter travelers of all, who, in 1854, on one of his extended explorations, discovered the ghastly truth concerning the final days of the Franklin expedition. Rae's report shocked the world with its horrifying revelations concerning the wretched demise of the expedition's last survivors and earned him the everlasting hatred of the Admiralty and the British geographical establishment.

The lesson of Franklin and Rae is clear: Once we embrace the outdoors as our home—however temporary—we can begin to enjoy a closer, more intimate relationship with the land. The more we know about our environment and the more we try to understand the wilderness, the more pleasurable they become.

Chapter 3

Groups and Leadership

Getting started in winter camping with a group is more fun and much safer than starting on your own. Group camping brings people together; the close interaction of a winter camping trip opens the way for mutual understanding and respect. Often, lasting bonds of friendship form between people who share the fun, laughter, and struggles of a winter wilderness experience.

The most important factors to keep in mind when forming a group are goals, picking a team, group size, group skills, judgment, and leadership. The most effective groups consist of people who willingly contribute their own special skills and assets toward a common goal, thereby making the group stronger and more experienced than any of the individuals in it. The whole group thus contributes to each member's strength, confidence, and knowledge.

As long as the members work together, the group functions well—but group dynamics are volatile, and the literature of outdoor adventure is replete with stories of groups that disintegrated when goals became confused and personalities clashed. Even the most talented groups exist only as long as the individual members are willing to subordinate personal desires and work toward mutual goals.

For any group to be successful, an agreed-upon mission or goal is essential. If misunderstanding or disagreement about the goals and objectives of the trip develop once it has begun, you're in for a rough time.

An important part of the planning process is to have a meeting of all prospective group members. Everyone should express just what it is he or she hopes to accomplish on the trip. Goals may be different: One person may want to traverse a mountain range, while another wants to make a base camp and take pictures. Now, at this meeting, rather than later, is the time to settle any concerns and form a consensus.

Picking a Team

Unquestionably, picking your teammates is the most important pretrip decision. The wilderness has a way of bringing out a person's true character. If someone is selfish, moody, or short-tempered, the stresses of a camping trip will spotlight these flaws. Likewise, if your fellow group member is responsible, cheerful, and fun to be with, these traits will be apparent.

If you can, travel with people you trust and know well. Many groups, once formed, take trips together year after year. Like a team on the playing field, members anticipate each other's reactions. They've learned to work together and succeed.

Perhaps you know people whose company and skills you've enjoyed in a summer camping group. In any case, there must be a basis of trust. Compatible group members must make decisions that instantly affect people's safety, often on the basis of incomplete knowledge. You can't avoid the people you travel with day after day, but must make every effort to get along as well as possible.

My friend Dan once returned from an expedition in which the group members were highly incompatible: "We never really meshed as a group,"

Toboggans can be easily pulled whether you're skiing or, as here, snowshoeing.

he said. "So after the trip we did the next best thing: We split into six groups of one. After that, we got along fine—no hassles! Six different dinner reservations, six cabs to the airport. . . ."

Group Size

What size group is best? Four might be the ideal number. In the event of an accident, one person can attend to the injured member while two go for help. Four is an easy number to cook for: A good-sized one-pot meal will amply serve four, but may be on the skimpy side for five or six.

Putting four people in one vehicle is probably the most cost-efficient way to travel. Getting more than four people and all their gear into the average car is like trying to see how many people you can stuff inside a phone booth.

Six people can be a lot of fun, but groups of more than six may lose the team feeling that's so desirable on a winter outing. With more than six, there may be too many variables—more personalities, needs, desires, and abilities. The chances for incompatibility among the members increase as group size grows. Also, large groups may have a negative impact on the environment, exceeding the carrying capacity of an area or possibly destroying the sense of solitude and space. The ideal group size may be no fewer than four and possibly no more than six.

Of course, the ideal is not always attainable, and you may have to scramble to find a third member when people back out at the last minute. Don't cancel your trip if a person drops out; just be aware of the increased risks, and take greater care to avoid problems.

Group Skills

One of the great advantages of traveling in groups is that each individual need not be expert at everything, as long as at least one person in the group has a necessary skill. One member may be a super skier, another highly skilled at ice travel. A third person may be a great outdoor cook, while a fourth is a genius with map and compass. By recruiting individuals with different strengths, the entire team gains in proficiency. The trip becomes more interesting if teammates can learn from each other and share their skills along the way. Just be sure that all the critical skills, such as first aid and navigation, are well represented.

Judgment

Judgment is an intangible but essential quality that far outweighs any combination of specific technical skills. High-tech skills are desirable, of course, if you've set out on a technically difficult trip, but proficiency is an asset only when it's guided by good judgment. Purely physical skills unguided by reason are like errant missiles: You don't know what damage is going to result.

Judgment means listening to—not ignoring—your doubts and fears. Judgment means knowing when it's safe to proceed and when it's prudent to retreat. Judgment is a calm, level-headedness that keeps you from straying too far outside your or your group's comfort zone.

Judgment results not only from experience, but also from careful attention to surroundings and events: the connection between a change in wind direction and a coming storm, fresh snow and unstable slopes, a hollow sound at the tap of a pole and thin ice. Some people are more receptive to these subtleties than others. These people make good trail partners. Seek them out. If you find them, stick with them.

Leadership

Ninety percent of the decisions made during a trip will be arrived at democratically. There is certainly no need for an autocrat to tell the group how far to travel each day, when to stop for lunch, or what to eat for dinner.

The group needs experienced leadership when there is disagreement over more serious matters, such as whether to cross a section of ice or bushwhack around it, whether to travel on a stormy day or stay in camp, or how to proceed in the event of an emergency. In these situations, experienced leaders can help the group make sound decisions concerning questions of safety.

Leaders are not necessarily the biggest, strongest, or most technically skilled members of the team, but they are people who are highly experienced and have demonstrated good judgment. Leaders can emerge when situations arise requiring special knowledge and skills. For example, one group member may have more experience with avalanche conditions than the rest of the team. In suspect terrain, that person should not hesitate to speak up and tell the others whether or not it's safe to continue. Leaders

The best winter camping groups are those in which members share goals and objectives for the trip.

must have the confidence and support of all members and must not be afraid to make tough decisions for the benefit of the group as a whole.

Leaders naturally keep an eye on the progress of the entire group, working diligently to insure the safety and satisfaction of the team. Leaders, in short, must possess good judgment, must be good communicators, and must be sensitive to group dynamics. They also must be generous, able to call on reserves of extra energy, and have patience and understanding.

Other Jobs

On expeditions, people enjoy having responsibilities, and they like to receive recognition for what they do well. As part of your planning, the group should consider making a list of different responsibilities and dividing them up so everyone has a job.

Assigning planning tasks will give everyone a sense of commitment and will also insure that everything gets done. Here are the planning jobs that need attention.

Researcher

The researcher gathers information concerning the details of the trip: when, where, and how far to go; permits; snow conditions; and other physical and regulatory details. The researcher also compiles the base map and locates bail-out options and contingency routes. He or she gathers a list of phone numbers—hospitals, state or provincial police, land management agencies—to use in the event of emergency. This list, plus a copy of the trip itinerary, should be left in the care of a responsible person who is not going along on the trip.

Treasurer

The treasurer handles the money. Every group needs an up-front financial commitment from its members so that food, equipment, and other important purchases can be made, permits can be secured, transportation can be arranged, and so forth. The treasurer estimates the costs of the trip, raises the funds from the group members, and acts as banker.

The treasurer also needs to consider how to compensate nonmonetary contributions such as use of a member's car for transportation. Also, somebody always ends up lending out a lot of expensive equipment that

Hard work on the trail pays off with stunning views.

gets a lot of hard use. This use should likewise be factored in to the overall cost of the trip, and the owners should be compensated.

In the interest of peace and harmony, all financial matters should be arranged equitably far in advance of the departure date, and the treasurer should keep accurate records of all revenues and expenses.

Menu Planner

This person solicits meal ideas from group members and creates a menu that's well suited to the physical rigors of a winter camping trip and is tasty, varied, and efficiently packaged. The menu planner, working with the others, also determines how much food is necessary for the trip. On the expedition, he or she may even keep track of the food supplies and notes what's being consumed and at what rate.

Equipment Manager

There should be no chance that two days into the trip the group discovers that some vital piece of equipment was never acquired or was left behind. The equipment manager, in consultation with the rest of the team, generates a list of group and personal equipment, sees that necessary items are purchased, and makes sure that all equipment makes it to the trailhead.

Naturalist/Historian

When someone learns about the human and natural history of the region, the trip takes on added interest. Knowing about the area you're passing through immeasurably enhances everyone's experience. The naturalist/historian may want to work with the team to incorporate into the trip itinerary sites of natural or historical significance.

Communications Director

During the planning process, one person can serve as the central information agency linking all the team members. The communications director makes sure that everyone is kept up to date on how planning is proceeding and makes sure that everyone knows what he or she needs to be doing. The communications director can also serve as photographer and/or journalist.

Photographer and/or Journalist

Group members and their friends will certainly be interested in records from the trip, and local newspapers or magazines may be interested if you can document your experiences.

It should be clear by now that every successful winter camping trip requires a lot of pretrip planning. Depending upon your goals and objectives, this stage of the process can take a few days or a couple of months. The process can be as formal or informal as you like—some experienced groups that have worked together in the past know just what to do without much formal organization. In small groups, one person wears many hats. All that really matters is that everything gets done before you head out the door.

When planning, start early to give the group enough time to nail down all the details. As with other projects, details make all the difference. Especially on serious expeditions into remote areas, once you have your base map, draw up a trip itinerary. For each day of travel, write down your intended campsite; the number of miles to travel; bail-out points; interesting natural or human features; hazards, if any, to watch for; and any other pertinent information. Leave space to include the daily menu, if you wish, and distribute a copy to everyone in the group.

Going Solo

The conventional wisdom is that you should never go camping alone in winter—but there are no absolutes in winter camping, and people do go alone, either by choice or by necessity. Most northern fur trappers work their lines alone all winter long, sometimes spending a week or more in very harsh conditions on each circuit.

Experienced travelers who feel sufficiently skilled and who are in possession of sound judgment sometimes elect to travel solo. There are no hard-and-fast rules, and traveling alone in the winter wilderness can be an intensely satisfying experience. Yet it's important to understand the risks involved before you set out on your own.

The solo traveler is completely self-reliant. In the event of accident or injury, there is no one to help and little chance of rescue. Extra caution is required during even the simplest tasks because the margin of safety is so slim. An ax cut, an injury from a fall, an avalanche—should these incidents happen while individuals are traveling with others, the group can probably keep the situation from becoming desperate, but if they happen to the solo traveler, the scenario becomes a grave one indeed.

When you travel solo, remember that everything takes much longer. No one shares the work, yet everything must still be done. Allow yourself plenty of time to perform camp chores, and because you'll probably be breaking trail by yourself, be conservative in estimating daily traveling distances.

Group and Individual Self-reliance

In our culture, wilderness is a place to get away from the impositions and complexities of modern society. In the wilderness we can enjoy an unusually high degree of personal freedom.

Still, travel in winter wilderness is not without risk. By its very nature, wilderness is beyond the power of human beings to control or pacify—and that's the way most backcountry travelers want it. But to enjoy it, group members must do what they can to make the trip a safe one. Too often, winter campers and mountaineers take for granted the availability of rescue. This laissez-faire attitude leads to relaxed planning; a false sense of security; and, ultimately, emergencies in which the individuals or groups involved must be rescued, sometimes with tragic results. Implicit in accepting the freedoms of the wilderness is a willingness to be self-reliant—to accept responsibility for any situation that may arise.

When you plan your trip, do so with the assumption that your group will take care of an emergency by drawing on its own resources. Factor this assumption into your choice of partners, route, equipment, and contingency plans. Rescues are always expensive, often expose rescuers to needless danger, and sometimes result in a clamor to close the backcountry to winter travel. Those who would like to see the winter wilderness remain open and free should plan on being careful and as self-reliant as possible.

Don't push on if your judgment is telling you to stop, and monitor the condition of the others in the group. All members should be honest with each other. If you're too tired to keep going or have reservations about the wisdom of a particular plan, speak up. Group members should be respectful of each other's opinions and feelings and should evaluate each situation as objectively as possible. Learn to distinguish between what you would like to accomplish and what is actually within the ability of the group.

Chapter 4

Before You Go

Okay, the hard part is over. You've pulled together a diverse and interesting group of people, chosen an exciting area to explore, gathered the information, and now you're finally ready to hit the trail!

Well, you're almost there, but not quite. Remember, details are the difference between success and disappointment, and there are a few factors left to consider before you sling on your pack and head out into the winter wild.

Be in Shape

First, you won't enjoy your trip if, after a mile of easy snowshoeing or skiing, you need to call the stretcher bearers. You don't need to be an Olympic athlete to be a winter camper, but you do need to be in good

Staying active year round will increase your enjoyment of winter travel.

shape. Not only will you enjoy the trip a whole lot more, but you also won't be a burden or a health risk to the group.

If you exercise regularly, you're probably in good enough shape for a winter camping trip. If you spend time in the outdoors on a year-round basis—hiking, canoeing, mountain biking, riding—being in excellent shape is already a natural part of your life, and you move with ease and grace from one season into the next. Urbanites who run, bike, spin, or play sports at least three or four times per week will be physically prepared to get the most out of their trip. Those who are not used to regular exercise should begin a program well in advance of the departure date.

Winterize Your Vehicle

On a –20-degree evening I once saw a group of weary, happy campers get back to the trailhead at the end of a great trip only to discover that the cold had been playing havoc with their car while they were out playing in the snow. Their battery was stone dead, and it was an hour's drive to the nearest town. Before you go, make sure that your car is in shape for the trip too.

Be sure to read the section on winter driving in your owner's manual, and give your car a basic tune-up before driving in the cold and snow. Check the following carefully.

• **Spark plugs.** These should be in good shape. Replace them if necessary. Plugs are among the first parts to go in cold temperatures. And remember: If your car is fuel injected, you don't need to pump the gas pedal before you start it. If you do, you risk flooding the engine and fouling the plugs.

• **Battery.** You'll want your battery at full power, so test it before you leave. Starting a cold battery at the end of a trip draws a lot of power all at once. If your battery is not in good shape, it may die at the trailhead, and you'll not be happy.

• **Antifreeze.** Be sure antifreeze is at full strength. People from the south should replace water with antifreeze before they head north.

• **Belts.** Check the condition and tension of the belts. Bring spares if you're heading to a remote area.

• **Oil.** Multiweight oils, such as 10W-40, are best because they are less viscous at low temperatures, making it easier for your engine to turn over in the cold. At superlow temperatures, even multiweight oil may be too sluggish for your car to start. In this case, you may have to warm your oil pan. You can use your camp stove to do this in an emergency.

● **Gasoline.** Cold temperatures can cause condensed water vapor to freeze inside your vehicle's fuel lines. There are two steps you can take to avoid this problem. First, leave your gas tank half full or more when you set out on the trail. If the trailhead is a long drive from the last gas pump, bring along a full plastic gasoline jug and empty it into your vehicle's tank before you head out on the trail. Second, use dry gas. The alcohol solution in dry gas mixes with the water in your tank and keeps the gas line from freezing. Small bottles of dry gas are available at almost every service station north of the Mason-Dixon line.

● **Washer fluid.** Slush and salty spray thrown by other cars and trucks can make your ride to the trailhead hazardous. Be sure to top off your reservoir, and bring along an extra jug of washer fluid for the return trip.

● **Windshield wiper blades.** Winter blades are much better than standard blades for driving in snowy conditions and are available at service stations throughout snow country.

● **Snow tires.** These are a must where heavy snow conditions prevail. The deep tread of true snow tires bites into the snow and hangs on tightly. If you put them on all four wheels, you'll feel much more control. In recent years, all-season radials have replaced snow tires in all but the snowiest parts of the United States and Canada. These are not adequate for driving in snow country.

● **Four-wheel drive.** If you live in snow country or often drive on unplowed logging roads to get to a winter trailhead, consider using a four-wheel-drive vehicle. Four-wheel drive is now available on many road cars as well as trucks

Be sure your vehicle is in shape for winter travel.

and jeeps. Having all four wheels churning is a big help when you face a long drive through heavy snow, and it makes driving in winter conditions much safer. As with any vehicle, adding snow tires greatly increases your traction.

In addition to winterizing your vehicle, be sure to have the following items in your car.

- **Car shovel.** You'll be bringing a shovel or two on your trip, and they're very handy to have along for the drive. If you end up in a snow bank, they'll make getting out much easier.

- **Ice scraper**

- **Sack of sand or gravel.** If you hit glaze or glare ice, you'll have no traction. A small sack of sand can provide you with just enough grip to allow your vehicle across these treacherous sections.

- **Tube sandbags.** Placing several heavy (70-pound) tubular bags of sand in the bed of your pickup truck or the cargo area of your SUV greatly adds to the vehicle's stability in slick road conditions.

Safe Winter Driving

Here are a few winter driving tips.

- **Slow down.** The leading cause of all crashes in some snow-belt states is driving too fast on winter roads.

- **Avoid cruise control.** Do not use cruise control while driving in a storm or on slippery roads.

- **Allow safe driving distance between vehicles.** Do not closely follow the vehicle in front of you. Leave at least three car lengths between you and the car in front.

- **Watch for black ice.** Keep a sharp eye out for this ice on what appears to be dry pavement.

- **Know your vehicle.** If you drive a four-wheel-drive vehicle, do not overestimate the vehicle's capabilities on ice and snow.

- **Know the safe speed limit for the driving conditions.** During a winter storm, the following speeds are suggested: 45 miles per hour on an interstate highway, 40 miles per hour on U.S./state highways, and 35 miles per hour on rural roads or lightly traveled state highways. Remember that these are suggested limits only. Always drive carefully and according to actual road conditions.

Final Details

Before you leave, there are a few final details to consider.

Financial Matters

Consider for a moment how you'll cover the expenses you incur while on your trip, such as gas, tolls, shuttle fees, last-minute equipment purchases, hotels, and meals. Once in the wilderness, you'll have no use for money, but what will you do with any money you need before, during, and after your trip? You can carry cash, but you may feel vulnerable carrying large sums of money, and there will be opportunities for it to get lost or misplaced if you aren't careful.

Major credit cards are accepted just about everywhere these days, and ATM machines are ubiquitous, so plastic may be the best solution to the money problem. An added advantage for Americans paying with credit cards in Canada is that you're billed at the actual rate of exchange (which is often favorable), rather than at the reduced rate offered by most merchants.

Also, if you're an American going to Canada, and you plan on using cash, the group's treasurer should be sure to convert your American money to Canadian currency at an American bank to ensure that you receive the most favorable exchange rate. Of course, Canadians traveling to the United States should do the same. Canadians will find that some merchants in the northern states compete for their business and will take their money at par with American currency, even if the exchange rate is unfavorable to them.

Vehicle Shuttle

If you plan a long-distance linear route, you'll need to arrange transportation back to your point of origin, or you'll need to find someone to shuttle your vehicle to your final destination. In some national parks or other popular camping areas, there are backpacker and skier shuttles that will carry you and your equipment for a small fee. In more remote areas, call the local chamber of commerce. Often local guides or outfitting services will be happy to shuttle your vehicle for you. The fee is usually reasonable and the time saved can be spent on your trip, not in the car.

Car Keys

Be sure you know who has the car keys. On one trip I made, we got to our final destination only to discover that the person who was supposed to have the keys had left them at our starting point. Nobody was particularly happy with this discovery.

The problem could have been easily avoided if we simply carried a spare set of keys or if we'd placed a set in a small magnetic box hidden somewhere underneath the car, on the car's frame or trim. If you have your vehicle shuttled, be sure both you and your driver understand where the keys will be left.

Personal Trip Journal

It always amazes me how many vivid details, memories, and feelings come back when I reread a journal from one of my trips. A journal keeps your memories fresh when they would otherwise dissipate and blur over time. The extraordinary sights, activities, personal interactions, and insights that you experience on a winter camping trip are worth preserving.

The journal need not be a chore. A typical entry can be as short as a few terse facts jotted in haste. Even these few details will trigger your memory of other events, bringing a flood of remembrances and helping you to re-create the sequence in detail.

Camera

Documenting your trip digitally or on film is one of the best ways to preserve the memories. A picture reveals at a glance what might otherwise take pages to describe. A carefully chosen sequence of images can tell the story of your trip, allowing you to relive it again with friends and family. Also, sponsors, newspapers, or magazines may have an interest in your photos if they're of high enough quality and reveal important information.

Snow School

What is the southernmost point in the United States where has snow fallen?

Snow fell in Homestead, Florida, outside of Miami, on January 19, 1977. •

Plan on shooting a great deal. Even if you aren't a photographer, you'll find that the images, enhanced by your written journal notes, will keep the trip fresh for years to come.

Equipment Checks

Now is the time to be sure that all your equipment is in good shape and won't fail when you need it most. Be sure everyone has proper clothing, footwear, and sleeping gear. Check all items, making sure that rips are sewn, seams are waterproofed, screws are tightened, and bindings are adjusted. Be sure that the tents are in good repair and that no poles are missing. All the food should be purchased and packed and all group cooking gear should be accounted for.

Check the stoves. Start them and make sure they burn properly. Every group member should practice firing up the stoves before he or she has to operate them in the cold. Make sure that everyone understands the basics of stove repair. When tools malfunction in the cold, knowing how to fix them quickly is a highly desirable skill.

Check the Weather Forecast

You'll want to know in advance if it's going to be clear or if a major storm is going to pound you. You may choose to delay your start or make a contingency plan. Often, heavy snow will not stop but only delay you. If so,

It's important to keep yourself hydrated on the trail. Drink lots of fluids.

Summary Planning Checklist

- [ ] Choose teammates.

- [ ] Assign planning chores.

- [ ] Pick an area to explore.

- [ ] Locate sources of information.

- [ ] Gather maps.

- [ ] Make a base map.

- [ ] Mark your route.

- [ ] Pencil in critical information.

- [ ] Plan for contingencies.

- [ ] Obtain permits.

- [ ] Winterize your vehicle.

- [ ] Check the weather forecast.

- [ ] Hit the road!

adjust your schedule and let people know you may be leaving and returning a day or two later than anticipated. If you're traveling in avalanche country, you may decide on an alternate route. Check the five-day outlook for the area in which you'll be traveling.

Hit the Road!

By now, you know that a winter camping trip consists of three parts—planning the trip, the trip itself, and learning from your successes and mistakes after the trip. For now, though, the planning is over and everything is ready to go. The team has been gathered, the car is packed, and it's time to hit the road and get to the trailhead.

Winterlude: The Myth of Words for Snow

A popular and long-lived myth suggests that Eskimos have 50 or 100 or perhaps even 500 words for different types of snow. This belief is so widespread that even the paper of record, the New York Times, *passed it on in an editorial entitled "There's Snow Synonym" about the Winter Olympic Games on February 9, 1984: "The prospect of snow must chill the hearts of television weather forecasters, as well as writers covering the Winter Olympic Games in Sarajevo, because there does not seem to be any short, acceptable synonym for 'snow.' . . . It's enough to make us envy the Eskimos. Benjamin Lee Whorf, the linguist, once reported on a tribe that distinguishes 100 types of snow and has 100 synonyms."*

Balderdash! First, there is no one Eskimo language. A number of cultures in Canada and Greenland refer to themselves as "Inuit," but there are actually five different Eskimo languages, such as Yupik in Alaska, that have their own words to describe the weather and weather-related phenomena.

Second, Whorf never made any such exaggerated claim. He suggested there were perhaps seven words for snow in the Inuit language.

So, Where did the myth come from? Not from native speakers, nor from linguists studying the native languages spoken around the circumpolar north. In a 1986 article in American Anthropologist, *Laura Martin traced the development of the myth from 1911, when the renowned Franz Boas declared that Eskimos used four words for snow. Later, in 1940 Whorf cited those seven words, and the number just kept growing out of control from there.*

The myth grew in part because different forms of the same word were being counted as individual words. For example, it's as if we considered "speak, speaks, spoke, and spoken" as unrelated words with completely different meanings.

Theories abound as to why the myth has been so universally accepted, but perhaps the most reasonable explanation is the notion that, because Eskimos are widely believed to be more in tune with their natural environment than the rest of us, they somehow view snow very differently than people from other cultures do.

It makes a certain amount of sense that those immersed in a particular environment will have more words to describe their surroundings, but is the New York Times *correct when it asserts there is no synonym in English for* snow?

I personally use approximately 80 words for snow, some interchangeably to describe conditions I encounter regularly—but I also admit that, unlike an editorial-page writer in a Manhattan skyscraper, I actually get out and spend time in the white stuff!

continued

Winterlude: The Myth of Words for Snow, continued

How many words do you have for snow? My personal vocabulary includes these:
Blizzard. A long-lasting storm with intense snowfall accompanied by high winds.
Blue ice. Snow that has melted, refrozen, and compacted so completely that the sur-
face feels rock hard.
Boilerplate. The same as blue ice.

Telemarking in thick, wet Alaskan glop. Shall we call it Chugach chowder?

Bullet-proof. Ditto.

Cascade concrete. Thick, heavy, sloppy, wet new snow common to the Pacific Northwest.

Champagne. Light and dry powder snow.

Cold smoke. Very cold, light, and dry powder snow.

Corn. Spring snow favored by skiers for the smooth, moist, yet firm surface provided by the coarse, granular snow crystals.

Cream cheese. Fresh, soft snow that has more moisture content than powder yet still has little cohesion.

Creeping snow. A snowpack on a steep slope that is stretching due to the pull of gravity.

Crud. Soft, mushy, heavy spring snow.

Crust. A frozen surface usually overlaying softer, drier snow.

Death cookies. These are fist-sized chunks of ice sometimes encountered in the back-country, but more often at ski areas.

Depth hoar. Large, faceted, angular, cup-shaped crystals at the bottom of the snow-pack, close to the ground. They are usually formed in the early winter when there's a greater difference between the ground temperature and the surface temperature.

Diamond dust. A type of frozen precipitation made up of tiny ice crystals that ap-pear to float slowly in the air on cold, cloudless days.

Dumping. It's dumping when snow is falling at the rate of 1 inch or more per hour.

Dust on crust. Loose, dry snow that falls on an icy or crusty surface.

Dusting. A very light snowfall.

Equi-temperature snow. Snow crystals that become rounded and well-bonded due to the lack of a large temperature differential in the snowpack.

Faceted snow. Snow crystals that metamorphose into grains at a fast rate due to a large temperature gradient in the snowpack. The grains then become faceted and bond poorly, thereby creating a significant avalanche hazard.

Firn. Snow that is at least a year old but which has not yet consolidated into glacier ice. It has a dry, Styrofoam feel.

Firnspiegel. An ice crust that forms on the surface of the snowpack on cold, sunny days. As the sun's heat penetrates the surface, it causes the grains beneath the sur-face to melt, but the moisture at the surface refreezes immediately, forming a thin layer of ice.

Fish-case snow. Corn snow in the early morning, before it's warmed. It looks and feels like the "snow" seafood is laid out on in supermarket cold cases.

Flurries. A light, brief snowfall, usually with little accumulation.

Formica. Essentially the same rock-hard snowpack as blue ice and boilerplate.

continued

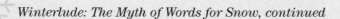

Freshies. *Newly fallen snow that has not yet been tracked by skiers.*

Frost. *The white, thin, crystal covering of ice that forms on exposed surfaces when the temperature falls below freezing.*

Frozen granular. *A term skiers use when machine-made snow cover has turned to ice.*

Glacial fire. *Another term for firnspiegel.*

Gliding snow. *Wet spring snow cover moving at a slow glide (from several inches to several yards per day) down a smooth slope. As the snow glides, widening glide cracks may appear in the snow cover.*

Glop. *A term for conditions similar to Cascade concrete and Sierra cement, but without the regional specificity.*

Golden corn. *Mature corn snow that's become fat, moist globules.*

Granular. *A term used by skiers to describe machine-made snow as it warms up and starts melting.*

Graupel. *Small, round pellets like ball bearings that form when freezing fog condenses on a snowflake, forming a little white ball of rime ice. Also known as snow pellets.*

Ground blizzard. *Occurs when strong winds lift and swirl loose snow that has already fallen, often creating large drifts and whiteouts.*

Hail. *Ice balls that normally range from the size of a pea to the size of a golf ball, although in rare instances they can be much larger.*

Hardpack. *Snow that has been packed firmly, usually by skiers, and yet is carveable and is not ice.*

Hard slab. *A dense, cohesive layer of snow most frequently formed by wind compaction.*

Hoarfrost. *Composed of ice crystals that form when water vapor from the atmosphere condenses directly into the solid phase onto a very cold surface.*

Ice needles. *The same as diamond dust.*

Lake-effect snow. *When cold winds move across long expanses of warm lake water, they pick up water vapor, which then freezes and is deposited as snow on downwind shores and mountains.*

Mashed potatoes. *Warm, thick, deep, sloppy snow that is tough to ski in.*

Mank. *Wet, grabby, granular snow that forms on overcast, unusually cool but not freezing days in the spring.*

Melt-freeze crust. *A hard, generally thin, icy top layer of the snowpack that forms during the melt-freeze process, usually in the spring. Often melt-freeze crust is firm* enough to support a traveler in the morning, before the warmth of the day softens the surface.

Mixed crud. Thick, freshly fallen snow that has been heavily cut by skiers and snowboarders.

Mixed precipitation. A combination of snow, sleet, and freezing rain.

Neve. The same as firn.

Orographic lift snow. Occurs when wind pushes humid air up mountain slopes. As the air rises, it cools, and the water vapor it contains begins condensing into snowflakes. As the air continues to flow over the mountains, it creates locally heavy snowfall at higher elevations.

Packed powder. Old powder snow that has been on the ground long enough to harden and compress, yet is still loose enough to edge with a ski.

Packing snow. Snow at the melting point that is perfect for snowball fights and other winter games, such as building snow forts and quinzhees (Athabaskan snow houses) and for making snowmen.

Pellet snow. The same as graupel.

Penitentes. Blades or spikes of snow or ice commonly found on high-altitude glaciers. Formed in the clear, dry air through sublimation, they can be 12 feet or greater in height.

Perennial snow. Snow that persists on the ground year after year.

Powder. Light, dry, freshly fallen, loose and uncompacted snow.

Pow pow. A skier's term for powder snow.

Puking. A skier's term for snow that is falling and accumulating at a rapid rate, usually at an inch per hour or more. The same as dumping.

Red snow. A reddish or pink-colored snow sometimes found at high altitudes. The color is caused by algae.

Rime. A deposit of white ice formed by the rapid freezing of supercooled water droplets that contact exposed objects.

Sastrugi. Eroded, sculpted, wind-carved shapes of snow that resemble small, sharp sand dunes and form parallel to the prevailing wind direction.

Scratch. The surface layer of hard snow that is exposed when wind blows away all loose surface snow. Its texture is between that of hardpack and boilerplate.

Seasonal snow. There are two definitions: (1) snow that accumulates during the course of one season and (2) snow that lasts for only one season.

Sierra cement. Essentially the same as Cascade concrete, just farther south.

Sleet. Small ice pellets that form when snowflakes fall through a shallow layer of

continued

warm air. The flakes thaw and then refreeze as they exit the warm air and reenter colder air near the surface of the earth.

Slush. *Partially melted, wet snow on the ground.*

Snow burst. *A very intense, brief snowfall.*

Snow devil. *A swirling tornado consisting of wind-driven newly fallen or loose snow. Often 20 to 50 feet high, snow devils form on flat, open snowy surfaces such as lakes and fields.*

Snow squall. *A brief but very intense snowstorm that may deposit significant accumulated snow. Similar to a snow burst.*

Snowstorm. *A long-lasting storm of relatively heavy snow.*

Soft slab. *A layer in the snowpack consisting of low-density snow that is deposited under calm or light wind conditions.*

Spindrift. *Dry, light snow picked up, blown about at the surface level, and then deposited elsewhere by the wind.*

Sugar snow. *The same as depth hoar.*

Suncups. *Scooped depressions in the snow caused by intense sunshine melting the surface of the snowpack.*

Surface hoar. *The same as hoarfrost.*

Sweet corn. *Young corn snow; snow that's in the early stages of transitioning to corn.*

Thundersnow. *A thunderstorm that produces snow as the primary form of precipitation.*

Temperature-gradient snow. *The same as depth hoar.*

Trap crust. *A melt-freeze crust that previously supported your weight but that has warmed to the point that you occasionally break through, even on skis.*

Uplift snow. *Same as orographic lift snow.*

Verglas. *A thin coating of very clear ice.*

Watermelon snow. *The same as red snow.*

Whiteout. *A weather condition in which snow-diffused daylight combines with an overcast sky to create opaque lighting in which contrast vanishes and the traveler is unable to distinguish either the horizon or any surface features.*

Wind-blown. *Essentially the same as scratch.*

Windpack. *The hard surface of soft snow formed by the action of the wind compacting the snow.*

Chapter 5

Gear for Camping

You don't need to spend a fortune outfitting yourself for winter camping, at least not if you don't want to. Marketing people are skilled at creating needs when essentially what they are really doing is tapping into your desires. If you want to save money, be conservative when buying equipment: Buy the best-quality item you can afford; you don't need an equipment failure halfway through your trip, but don't get something until you absolutely need it.

You can borrow from friends or adapt what you already have—and if the item is not critical, make do without it so that you can solve the cash-flow problem and live by Thoreau's timeless dictum: "Simplify, simplify, simplify." It's a lot less hassle, and you'll be sure not to insulate yourself from your experience and your surroundings with piles of useless stuff.

On the other hand, the proper gear used with skill can extend your abilities beyond limits. So purchase what you need and leave the rest behind.

You're going to need a few selected items to get you out into the winter wild. But before you run out to the shop and get outfitted, there are a few questions you should ask yourself: Will you be skiing or snowshoeing? Do you want to travel fast and light through rugged terrain or take a more leisurely trip over easy trails? Are you headed into the subarctic, or will temperatures be a bit more moderate? Asking these questions now can help you sort through the equipment choices and ensure that you get what you need. In this chapter, we'll discuss equipment for camping and travel. Because clothing is a big subject, we'll deal with it in the next chapter.

Packs

People have hauled loads on their backs since the beginning of time. The difference between earlier times and now is that today's packs have sophisticated padding and suspension systems, allowing even the heaviest, most unwieldy load to ride comfortably on your back. For winter campers, especially those who climb mountains or ski the hills and forest trails, the new pack designs have meant a welcome increase in freedom of movement and maneuverability.

An overnight pack for the winter backcountry must be big enough to carry your food, clothing, and equipment. The pack must be tough enough to withstand the stresses of bushwhacking and climbing, and it must be comfortable, stable, and designed to allow you to move freely, unencumbered by awkward extensions or rigid attachments. Finally, the pack must have the necessary systems to secure on skis, ice axes, and other winter equipment on the outside, where they're easily accessible to the mittened hand.

There are three basic types of backpacks: the external frame pack and internal frame pack, for carrying big loads, and the daypack, a small, lightweight pack for day trips or side trips on longer journeys.

External Frame Packs

These are the classic big backpacks that you almost never see anymore. They are large, multicompartmented, and attached to a rigid outer frame. The rigid frame gives you excellent control over heavy loads by placing the weight high on your shoulders and in line with your spine, thereby putting most of the burden on your skeletal system and less on your muscles. The frame also holds the pack bag away from your back, allowing air to circulate more freely, which keeps your back cooler and drier. These packs also simplify gear organization by offering an array of dividers in the pack bag and the outside pockets. For carrying heavy or awkward loads over moderate terrain, an external frame is an excellent tool for the job.

There are numerous disadvantages to this type of pack for winter camping, however. External packs reduce your freedom of movement and range of motion while climbing or skiing. The high center of gravity that's so advantageous while hiking can throw off your balance. Because external packs are worn off your back, they tend to side slip when you rotate your torso, rather than rotate with you. In practice, this means that when you turn one way, your pack keeps going the other.

The side pockets of external frame packs can also be a problem: Though they're advantageous for organizing your pack, they restrict your poling; your arms tend to strike them on the backswing. The tall frame on these packs can also be a monster: It keeps you from being able to look up, it can catch on branches when you're bushwhacking, and it may bang you on the back of the head when you take a fall.

Even so, many winter campers who know the pros and cons put up with the disadvantages of these packs in the interest of economy, preferring to use their summer external frame packs and avoid the added expense of buying a special winter pack.

Internal Frame Packs

These packs are much preferred by winter campers and have all but replaced external frame packs. Internal frame packs have stiff stays of metal, plastic, or synthetic fiber inserted into the fabric of the pack, and these stays provide a narrow internal frame that can be shaped to the contours of your back. Packed correctly, the load itself also provides stability. The advantages of internal frame packs for winter use are numerous. They give increased freedom of motion by holding the load close to your body, snugging it tight so that it conforms to your shape. This allows the pack to turn and twist with you, making it much more maneuverable for skiing and climbing. The lower center of gravity keeps you well balanced on rough or uneven terrain, and the compact shape of the pack neither interferes with poling nor gets hung up in brush when you're bushwhacking.

An internal frame pack can handle the weight you have to carry in the winter.

One disadvantage of the internal frame pack is the care you must use when packing it. Because the pack is snug and formfitting, any haphazardly packed item will press against your back and annoy you. Another disadvantage is the lack of air circulating behind your back to keep you cool and dry. (When it's really cold, this pocket of air can be an advantageous extra layer of insulation.) With some internal frame packs, you can add a foam pad to the lumbar region to make the pack more comfortable. Finally, the major disadvantage is the higher cost of internal frame packs—though there are many good packs that cost less, top-of-the-line expedition packs can cost several hundred dollars.

Daypacks

Daypacks are handy to bring along for day hiking or touring once you've set up a base camp. They're usually large enough for extra clothing, lunch, a water bottle, a first aid kit, and other accessories.

What to Look for in a Pack

If you're going to be carrying home on your back for a while, make sure you have the features you need. A pack that doesn't have the capacity, doesn't fit properly, or is lacking in needed accessories can threaten your enjoyment of your trip. Here are a few features to look for when choosing a pack.

A daypack is handy for snowshoeing or ski touring from a base camp or hut.

Size

Get a pack that's large enough to carry the additional bulk of winter gear, including fluffy jackets, hefty sleeping bags, food and fuel for several days, and so on. Of course, there seems to be an unwritten law of backpacking that requires you to fill any available space to the limit, but if you have a large pack, you'll have ample room for everything you need for a multiday trip. A pack of 5,000 cubic inches (different manufacturers measure capacity differently) or larger will do the job.

Suspension System

You'll be carrying about 80 percent of the full pack's weight on your hips. Therefore, it makes sense to buy a pack with a comfortable, effective, and adjustable hip belt. Shoulder straps—which stabilize and support the load, keeping it close to your back and responsive to your motions—should also be comfortable and easily adjustable, letting you move the pack away from or closer to your back. Make sure the pack you're preparing to purchase has a sternum strap, which helps keep the load stable and responsive to movement. All of these straps should be well padded, and you should be able to adjust them while moving and wearing mittens.

Compression Side Straps

These straps are sewn into the sides of the pack and are useful for compressing the load and keeping it from swaying or bouncing around. They also bring the load in snug to your back. Additionally, when you don't need your poles, you can carry them by sliding them through the compression straps alongside the main compartment of the pack.

Accessories

Most packs come with some desirable extras, such as tabs for lashing on equipment, extendable top pockets for increased pack capacity, removable top pockets that convert to large-volume belt packs, ski holsters for securely carrying skis, ice-ax loops, snow-shovel pockets, lumbar pads contoured to fit into the small of your back, and torso pads to cushion your back against the load. All of these features can increase your packing options and make your life easier. They'll also add to the cost of the pack.

Fit

Before you take a pack into the winter wild, make sure it fits you properly. Suspension systems are becoming so complex that we'll soon need certified technicians to help us figure them out. Be sure to try the pack on in the store under proper supervision and fill it with the kind of heavy, bulky items you'll bring on your trip. Simulate skiing, climbing, and snowshoeing motions. Ask the store personnel to adjust the suspension system. How does it feel? Is it comfortable enough for an extended winter camping trip? How does it compare to the other packs in the store?

Packs fit men and women differently because of their different body shapes. Men tend to have longer torsos, while women have longer legs. There are now many women-specific packs, so make sure you get a pack that is designed for your body shape. Also, while fitting the pack, men should place heavy items higher in the pack, because their center of gravity is up near the chest, while women should place the heavier items lower, near their center of gravity in the abdominal area. Both men and women can carry heavier loads more comfortably if the weight is placed properly.

Sleds

For years I adapted summer backpacking techniques to winter, traveling fast and light in the mountains, unencumbered by lots of gear. As the years passed, however, I started taking longer, more ambitious trips deeper into the wilderness, and I realized the backpacking paradigm didn't always work very well. This lesson came home to me while I was packing for a multiday trip to Maine's remote Mount Katahdin, deep in Baxter State Park.

If it's true, as the ancient philosopher wrote in *The Art of War,* that every battle is decided before it's fought, then I knew I was in for a good thrashing. I stood in the basement, knee deep in gear, staring bleakly at the piles of equipment strewn about the floor. Everywhere I looked there were tents, sleeping bags, camp stoves, fuel bottles, ice axes, crampons, ropes, mounds of food, clothes, and other odd but essential items.

While roving over this chaos, my eye fell upon my backpack. It was so pitifully unequal to the task of hauling all that stuff up to Katahdin that I burst out laughing. No, it would never do. Even when the pile was split between several people, it would be too large to carry on our backs. I sat down on a soft pile of nylon and down and looked around at what now seemed a mountain of gear. "This isn't going to work," I thought. "There has to be a better way."

Not only was the load too huge, but also, as anyone who has ever tried it knows, skiing with a heavily overloaded pack is ungainly. Just thrust out your hips a touch and over-rotate your shoulders while cutting a turn and

For larger and heavier loads, use a sled.

whoops! There you go, swooping out of control, arms and legs churning like eggbeaters, only to land face first in a snow crater of your own design. And going uphill, all that weight driving you into the snow like a nail is equally unpleasant if less dramatic.

With that bleak prospect before us, my companions and I were sufficiently inspired to do some creative thinking. We soon came up with a plan to get our gear and ourselves to the mountain.

A couple of days later, we were skiing the trail to Roaring Brook. It was a beautiful, cold, crisp day. Our daypacks rode easily on our hips and shoulders, the sleds tugged steadily but not too heavily on our hip belts. That mountain of gear, so discouraging to contemplate in the basement, was riding comfortably on a convoy of sleds.

As usual when in a quandary, we had turned to the experts: the Indians and old-timers of the north. Originally, neither sleds nor toboggans were children's toys, though they served that purpose when the work was done. Instead, they were designed and used for hauling loads, and they've served well for thousands of years. What better way to haul cordwood, hides, game, or gear through heavy snow?

Skiing with a sled is sometimes hard work, but compared to skiing with a heavy pack, it can be blissfully easy. All the weight that you might have carried on your back is now sliding along behind you. Sleds are not the ideal solution in all types of terrain, but short of a team of huskies or a small army of porters, they do the job.

If you want to travel fast and light, you don't need a sled. Many winter campers prefer to go winter backpacking by adjusting their summer camping strategies to a winter environment. But if you want to take along the extras for added comfort or additional activity, if you want to set up a base camp from which to explore an area on day tours, or if you want to go deep into the wilderness on a lengthy expedition, then taking a sled is the way to go. With a sled you can carry your weight in food and equipment.

Toboggans

For traveling over level or gentle terrain, a sledding toboggan is perfectly adequate. The sledding toboggan is essentially the recreational version of the sleds used for millennia by Indians in the northern forests. The Indian toboggan is narrower, perhaps 10 or 12 inches wide at the front and tapering to 6 or 8 inches wide at the rear. The tapering shape actually makes the toboggan track better.

The Indian toboggan is also quite a bit longer than the recreational sled (10 feet or more in length), and the front curl is curved higher, allowing the Indian toboggan to plow through deep drifts.

A toboggan can be easily hauled by attaching a loop of cord or climbing webbing to the front at the base of the curl. Throw the loop over one shoulder and under the opposite arm and you're ready to pull.

Load your toboggan by placing the bulk of the weight slightly toward the rear to keep the front of the toboggan above the snow. Place a soft duffel bag, a plastic tarp, or a nylon or cotton tarpaulin on the toboggan, and then load your food and equipment. Make sure no items are wider than the toboggan so that they can't catch on branches, roots, and rocks. If an item is wider than it is tall, place it on end when you load it. When all items are placed on the toboggan, lash the load securely so that nothing spills out during the day. The sled should be able to turn over and not lose or shift the load.

For tours on rolling or uneven terrain, it's advisable to have rigid bars connecting you to the sled so it doesn't run up on your heels during a descent. Also, runners on the bottom help the sled to track behind you, keeping it from zigzagging or sliding off a slanted trail.

Molded Plastic Sleds

You can make your own sled or buy a commercially manufactured one. The molded plastic sleds available for a few dollars at toy stores can be adapted to winter trips. They are tough, have slightly raised runners that help keep them tracking, and are very inexpensive. A 6-foot-long sled is big enough to haul food and gear for a substantial trip.

One way to adapt a toy-store sled to backcountry purposes: Drill holes at spaced, 10- or 12-inch intervals all around the top of the sled side walls. Then, beginning at the front of the sled, thread a length of polypropylene rope through the holes along one side, around the rear, and back to the front along the other side. Next, take the two ends of the rope emerging at the front of the sled and pass them through approximately 4 $\frac{1}{2}$-foot lengths of $\frac{3}{4}$-inch PVC pipe, which you can buy at any hardware store. The pipes should be long enough so that the sled stays well behind your ski tails on a descent or when you kick and glide on the flat. Tie loops in each end of the rope, clip a carabiner to each loop, and hitch the carabiners to the waist belt of a backpack or daypack loaded only with items you want to have handy during the day.

Crossing the pipes between your pack and the sled adds a lot of control on descents and when traveling on a trail with many twists and turns. To keep the pipes together, tie a loop of utility cord or clip a carabiner around the pipes where they cross. Now, for a total investment of about $25 and 30 minutes, you're ready to go.

Load your sled the way you would load the toboggan, by putting the heavier items low and slightly toward the rear to keep the sled from tipping and to keep the front of the sled from nosing into the snow. Some people simply place a duffel bag on the sled and fill it; others first put down a sled wrapper, such as a space blanket, and then place all of the items in the sled and wrap the load to keep out snow and moisture. Be sure to lash or bungee cord the load securely to the sled so that it doesn't come undone during the day.

Several of the commercial sleds are extremely well made—indestructible, lightweight—and come with a padded hip harness system that makes pulling them if not a pleasure, then a very efficient means of moving loads over long distances. The rigid harness, rigid bars, and aluminum runners give you a control that's impossible to match with homemade sleds. Commercial sleds come with attached covers and lashing systems that hold the load securely and protect it from moisture.

Sleeping Bags

One of the most important equipment decisions Will Steger had to make when planning his historic 1986 dogsled expedition to the North Pole was choosing a sleeping bag. He needed a bag with plenty of thickness, or loft, to withstand –70-degree temperatures; a well-designed shape to ensure efficient warmth-to-weight ratio; and a compact fill material that wouldn't collapse when wet.

This last point is especially important, because during the eight hours or so that we're asleep, our bodies expel water vapor—approximately 1 pint of water per night. This expelling of moisture, called insensible perspiration, occurs even when we aren't sweating but are merely at rest. Insensible perspiration passes from the body into the fill of the sleeping bag, compromising its insulation value.

Over the course of a multiday winter trip, a bag can accumulate this moisture and become saturated. In subfreezing temperatures, this means your bag will fill with ice if you don't take the time to dry it periodically.

Pressed for time, Steger was unable to stop and dry out his bag. By the end of the eight-week expedition, his bag weighed well over 50 pounds.

What kept Steger warm on his expedition was his decision to use a bag with 14 inches of loft. (The thicker the bag, the more ice could accumulate without total loss of warmth.) His bag also had a tapered-body, contoured, mummy shape to reduce heat loss, and it was filled with a synthetic fiber that became compact when packed and retained some insulation value even when sheathed in ice.

The North Pole may not be in your travel itinerary, but if you plan on camping in winter, you face the same choices regarding loft, fill, and shape that Steger did when he was putting together his outfit. You need a good night's sleep after a long day on the winter trail, and your sleeping bag can be either a warm, pleasant haven or a frigid cocoon. A sleeping bag is your last resort in bitter cold. As with other equipment, it pays to shop wisely in the sleeping bag department.

Choosing a Sleeping Bag

Before you run out and buy a sleeping bag, ask yourself some important questions. As with most winter camping equipment, it's important for you to decide how you plan to use it. Keep the answers in mind as you shop for the winter bag that matches your needs.

How important is weight? Some winter campers are fanatical about weight. They'll do whatever they must to shave a few ounces from their pack, even if it means getting up early every morning to dry their lightweight, down bags. Others, myself included, would rather put up with a little extra weight and sleep in.

How do you sleep? Some people are cold sleepers, shivering through the night in a high-loft winter bag while friends are snoring soundly in an identical bag. And what about the environment? Some winter campers travel in cold, dry climates, while others can expect a snowstorm one day followed by freezing rain the next. Your choice of bag should take into account these factors. Here are some sleeping bag features to look for.

Loft

How warm a bag is depends upon the thickness of the fill. The thicker the fill, the more dead air spaces are created to trap warm air.

Fills. Despite the development of new synthetics, goose down is still the warmest fill per given weight, providing about $\frac{1}{3}$ more insulation than the same amount of any high-tech synthetic fiber. The result is an equally warm bag for ⅓ less weight. Down also compresses more compactly than synthetics, providing equal warmth with less bulk. For a warm, light, small bag, down can't be beat. Also, if well maintained, down bags can last twice as long as fiber-filled bags. So why not skip the rest of this chapter and rush out now for a down bag? There are other considerations.

Down absorbs moisture rapidly, and the loft collapses when damp, rendering the bag a useless sack of wet feathers. Remember, moisture comes not only from external sources—melting snow, sleet, and rain—but also from your own perspiration and respiration. On the trail, you'll literally be pouring a pint or more of water into your bag every day. Unless the bag is scrupulously dried on a daily basis, this moisture may collapse it, leaving you out in the cold.

Synthetic bags retain much of their insulation value when wet, making them top performers in cold, wet, and snowy conditions. They also dry quickly, and a synthetic bag usually costs about half as much as a comparable down bag. The main disadvantage of a synthetic bag is the extra bulk and weight you'll have to carry—they can be up to 30 percent heavier and bulkier than comparable down bags.

Shape. There really is no choice here: When you're winter camping, go with a mummy bag. Although they're roomier, rectangular bags are much heavier and much colder. Mummy bags, which closely contour the body, are the most efficiently shaped sleeping bags, offering the most warmth. Mummy bags also have an insulated hood that can be drawn closely around the head to further keep the warm air inside the bag from escaping.

Also, look for a bag with a well-insulated draft tube that lies against the full length of the zipper to keep out cold air, and make sure the bag has an insulated collar that wraps around your neck to prevent the escape of warm air and the entrance of cold air.

Size. Make sure you get a bag that's comfortable but is neither too large nor too small for you. It should just fit you. Your body must generate extra heat to warm up empty air space, but if your bag is too small, its contoured shape will restrict your movement. A rule of thumb: If you're 6 feet tall or shorter, choose a regular length bag. If you are more than 6 feet tall, choose a long bag. If you choose a bag that's too short, you'll stretch it in an attempt to make it cover you. Doing this will flatten the bag and its insulation, thereby reducing its effectiveness. Sleeping in a bag that's too long means your feet will have to work hard to stay warm in all that empty space, so plan on wearing your booties to sleep if your bag is too long for you.

Temperature ratings. These figures are useful but far from precise because there's no industry-wide, standard rating system in place to compare the bags of different manufacturers. You may find one bag rated at 0 degrees that is perfectly warm and shiver the night away in another bag with the same rating. For comparison within a certain manufacturer's line, however, these figures can be helpful.

Another problem with temperature ratings is that different people have different metabolic rates. The bag you're comfortable sleeping in at –20 degrees may be an icebox for someone else. What can you do? Be conservative in estimating the warmth of your bag. Experiment in a controlled setting, such as the backyard or a local campground. If you aren't sure, go with a warmer bag—you'll rarely be sorry.

Instead of buying a winter bag, you can use a thin summer-weight sleeping bag inside of a three-season bag. Just make sure there's plenty of room for this layering. Though perhaps a more economical solution, this system may add bulk and weight to your load. Try it before you head out on a long trip.

Sleeping Bag Covers

Although most modern sleeping bags come with shells that are treated for water repellency, there are still times when a sleeping bag cover comes in handy. This waterproof and breathable fabric keeps your bag from getting wet from melting snow inside snow caves, from spindrift if you're sleeping under a tarp, or from the snow that people invariably drag with them into a tent. If you're sleeping out under the stars or on a high mountain ledge somewhere without shelter, a cover is essential.

The extra layer of fabric not only keeps moisture from penetrating your bag from the outside, but it also keeps wind from stealing your warmth, and it creates another layer to trap warm air.

Sleeping bag covers are not trouble free. The moisture expelled by your body during the night passes through your sleeping bag insulation, and some of this moisture condenses as frost when it reaches the outer layer of sleeping-bag fabric. Here you can easily see it in the morning and brush it off. With a sleeping bag cover, however, the moisture condenses as frost between the bag and the bag cover. Unless you're careful and brush it from the inside of the bag cover every day, this frost can work its way back into your sleeping bag, increasing the amount of moisture already present there.

Sleeping Pads

Keep in mind that snow-covered ground is cold and that whatever insulation your bag provides for your back will be crushed by your weight as you sleep. The result? You may be warm on top, but that cold ground will suck the warmth right out of you, keeping you shivering all night long.

What can you do? You can add some insulation between your sleeping bag and the ground—and the more, the better. An easy way to do this is to use a sleeping pad. There are three basic types: open-cell foam pads, closed-cell foam pads, and self-inflating pads.

• **Open-cell foam pads.** These are comfortable, lightweight, and inexpensive, but because open-cell foam pads compress easily, they need to be about four times as thick as closed-cell foam pads. These pads also absorb moisture like a sponge, and they're not very durable.

• **Closed-cell foam pads.** These don't compress as easily, which means you can go with a much thinner pad. On very cold nights, however, you'll want more insulation, so carry two of these pads on midwinter trips. Closed-cell pads aren't as comfortable as open-cell pads, but they don't absorb moisture.

Also in this sleeping-pad category is the shorty pad: a small (roughly 16 inches by 16 inches) piece of old closed-cell foam pad. The shorty pad is handy for sitting on during lunch breaks or standing on when taking a bucket bath.

• **Self-inflating pads.** The typical self-inflating pad doesn't really self-inflate; you do have to open a valve and blow it up. Nevertheless, it's the most comfortable and generally useful sleeping pad. These pads combine the comfort of open-cell foam and a waterproof cover and are extremely compact when deflated and rolled up. You must be careful not to puncture them, however; bring along a patch kit just in case.

• **Clothing and packs.** You can use your extra clothing and your pack to keep yourself off the cold ground. Putting your pack under your legs and feet adds insulation, while arranging a layer or two of insulated clothing under your head and shoulders will also add to the efficiency of your sleeping pad.

Some winter campers still opt for a traditional cotton wall tent.

Tents

Maine guide and peerless winter camper Garrett Conover is not impressed with the new generation of high-tech tents. "Tiny, super-light tents take on the look of sensory deprivation chambers," he says, "with the additional torture of possibly having to share such a space."

When Garrett goes into the winter woods, he takes along a 10-by-12-foot wall tent made of fine-weave Egyptian cotton; a lightweight, sheet-steel trail stove; and a pair of kerosene lanterns. The whole outfit weighs about 45 pounds, but Garrett says no one has ever complained once he or she was basking in the 65-degree heat on a cold winter night.

Garrett packs his tent on a Cree toboggan, where it rides securely alongside his other equipment and provisions. With this outfit, even a severe cold snap—"bragging cold," as he calls it—is spent in warmth and luxury.

Where you go determines what you need to bring. If you aren't headed into the mountains, there's no reason to be spartan. Leave the backpack behind, find a large tent with a collapsible wood-burning stove, and load it on the sled. On a cold winter night, you'll relish the warmth and extra space.

If you're traveling quickly or heading to the mountains on a ski or snowshoe trip, a truly lightweight shelter is what you need. Backpacking tents are portable vacation homes. Just whip the tent out of the stuff sack, set it up, and there you are—home for the night.

Most backpacking tents consist of two layers: a waterproof fly that stretches over a breathable inner canopy. This two-layer system is designed to keep the inside of the tent dry. The fly prevents moisture from entering the tent from the outside while water vapor from wet clothing, breathing, and perspiration passes from the inside of the tent to the outside through the breathable canopy.

If properly sealed and stretched close to the ground, the fly is effective in keeping out moisture. Not all moisture from the inside passes through the breathable canopy, however. Instead, when the temperature inside the tent is warmer than outside (a desirable situation), moisture condenses on the cold fabric and collects as frost on the walls and ceiling of the tent. When this happens, knocking the interior walls will trigger tiny blizzards—the price you pay for the additional 20 degrees or so of warmth that a tent provides.

Tents come in various shapes, sizes, and colors. Domes and pyramids offer the best use of space, are wind stable, and resist snow loading. They allow you to move around freely and sit face to face with your tent mates. Tents with an A-shaped frame, on the other hand, catch the wind, and they restrict your movement by forcing you to face front or back, never side to side. Also, the walls of A-frame tents always feel like they're hanging over your shoulder or in your face.

The best tents for winter camping are the four-season models. The walls of these tents are made of nylon panels that trap body heat; the floor is usually a high-sided, waterproof washtub design to keep ground moisture from penetrating. The poles are made of extra-strong aluminum, and there are plenty of lash tabs sewn onto the fly so you can secure the tent with guy lines in strong winds. A nice added feature is a removable vestibule for storing equipment under cover or for using a camp stove while you're snug in the comfort of your sleeping bag.

Make sure to get a tent that's large enough for comfort. With all the extra clothing of a winter outing, it helps to have extra space. I find that two people can live quite comfortably on a multiday trip in most three-person tents. Of course, you can squeeze in another person if you must, but then it can become quite cozy.

I prefer tent doors that open to the side. With doors that open to the front it's easier to track snow inside the tent. Also, I prefer the cross-ventilation and four-season versatility offered by a tent with a large no-see-um screened rear window rather than tubular snow tunnels, which I find I never use, even in the worst conditions.

Backpacking tents come in a full range of colors, and this can make a difference when you've been out on the trail for several days. The brightly colored tents filter the sunlight, adding a cheerful cast to the light inside the tent. Even when the day is overcast and gloomy, these bright colors have a way of creating a pleasing atmosphere.

Tarps

Tarps are extremely useful, simple, lightweight shelters for the winter camper. They weigh a lot less than tents and are a lot less bulky to carry. They can also be set up quickly just about anywhere.

To make a very simple tarp shelter, simply dig a rectangular trench in the snow that's slightly wider and slightly longer than you are. Stick your skis upright in the snow at either end, and string the tarp between the skis so that it covers the trench. Bury the ends of the tarp with the snow you've just excavated, and—voilà!—you now have a very warm, snug shelter from the elements. You can line the bottom of the snow trench with a space blanket and your sleeping pad. To make your tarp shelter virtually weatherproof, simply build snow walls at either end of the trench.

Stoves

Even if you plan on doing your cooking over a fire, you may want to pack along a stove. On stormy days you can cook with your stove right outside the tent while you remain snug in your sleeping bag. In the event of an emergency, a stove can boil water in minutes, leaving you free to attend to other business. And by using a stove, you can lessen your impact on a heavily used area. In some places, stove-only policies have been implemented to protect fragile environments from decades of poor fire-building practices.

For a winter camping trip, you'll want a tough, reliable, easy-to-use stove that puts out a lot of heat, operates in cold temperatures, and is simple to repair in the field. For mountaineers, weight is also a factor.

White gas stoves are the best for winter use. White gas is additive-free automobile gasoline and is highly volatile. Some of these stoves sound like jet airliners and burn like blowtorches—you can practically rob a safe with them. White gas burns very hot even when it's extremely cold out, is easily obtained in North America, and is relatively inexpensive. Coleman fuel and Blazo are a couple of trade names for white gas, and these can be purchased at any camping-supply or hardware store.

White-gas stoves must be pumped occasionally to maintain pressure inside the fuel tank, and they require priming with preheat fuel—minor chores that tremendously increase performance and heat output.

Although some winter campers cook inside their tents on stoves, this practice cannot be recommended. Carbon monoxide is a by-product of white-gas combustion—the noxious fumes have caused the demise of more than one Arctic explorer—and preheating the stove sometimes causes a flare-up capable of reducing your tent to a puddle of melted, toxic goo in seconds. Be careful.

Other fuels are available for camping, but few have as many advantages as white gas for the winter camper.

- **Unleaded automobile gasoline.** This is widely available and is less expensive than white gas, but check first to see if your stove can use it without becoming clogged by the additives. If so, it may be the best choice for you.
- **Kerosene.** This fuel burns hot, is inexpensive, and is widely available, but it's hard to light, is smoky, has a strong smell, and takes a long time to evaporate if spilled.
- **Butane.** This works terribly in the cold, and you must pack out the non-renewable, disposable canisters.
- **Propane.** This fuel burns well at subzero temperatures, but the bottles weigh 2 to 3 pounds apiece, a sufficient disincentive for most stove users.
- **Blended fuels.** These mixtures of butane and propane work better than straight butane in cold weather, but you're still stuck with lugging nonrenewable, disposable canisters.

When operating a stove on the snow, you'll find it has a tendency to melt the snow underneath, causing pots to tip over. One ingenious friend has solved this problem by bringing along an old license plate that he puts under the burner. The trick works. In any event, you'll need to insulate

A rider throws a wave of "cold smoke" as he heads downhill.

the burner from the snow with something; an extra pot top will also do the job.

A major deterrent to stove performance is wind. Most stoves come from the manufacturer with specially designed windscreens. Even so, placing the stove out of the wind during operation is a good idea. You can also position snow blocks around the stove to shelter it from the wind.

Most people carry their fuel in round, aluminum bottles specifically made for this purpose. The bottles are lightweight and unbreakable, and the caps are sealed with rubber gaskets to prevent them from leaking. Fuel bottles should always be placed upright (and away from food) in your pack or on your sled to keep from spilling. It's best to fill your stove through a small funnel with a screen for trapping the impurities that can clog your stove and impede its performance.

How much fuel should you bring? That depends upon how often you plan to use the stove, whether you need to melt snow for water, and how elaborate your meals are. A rule of thumb is to bring $\frac{1}{4}$ to $\frac{1}{2}$ cup of fuel per person per day. By keeping your stove well maintained, clean, shut off when not in use, and out of the wind, you can make a small amount of fuel go a long way.

Cooking Utensils

Two large nesting pots—one for the meal, the other for hot drinks—and a separate frying pan suffice for most groups. Make sure that both pots have covers to keep in the heat and keep out stray matter such as ashes or pine needles. Pack the pots and pans in a stuff sack designated for the purpose. If the pots nest one inside the other, you'll have an easier time packing and transporting them.

A pot grip (or a vise grip or multitool from the repair kit) is handy for grabbing pots and pans, and if you do a lot of cooking over a fire, a pair of leather work gloves is very useful.

When you're sledding and can afford the extra weight, consider bringing a lightweight reflector oven for baking in front of the fire. If your group has a talented baker, let him or her treat you to fresh-baked brownies, coffee cake, and muffins. Also, because cooking at high altitudes takes much longer than at sea level, those in the western states and provinces may want to pack along a small aluminum pressure cooker to speed up cooking and rehydration of dried foods. It can save up to $\frac{2}{3}$ cooking time by using pressurized steam, which means not only that you'll have more time to relax, but also that you can pack in less fuel.

A small, lightweight grill is useful for cooking along with using the frying pan over the fire or to keep food warm. Complete your kitchen set with a ladle, a serving spoon, a spatula, and a small whisk for mixing ingredients. Toss in a scrub pad for cleaning up.

For hot drinks, I like my insulated mug with the top that clamps on and keeps in the heat. If you're like me, though, you'll lose the top of this mug within a day or two if you don't punch a hole in the cover and tie it to the handle.

For eating, bowls work best on the winter trail. You can use them for soups, stews, pastas, and other meals without worrying about the food spilling or getting cold. A bowl can do everything a plate can do and is much more practical in the outdoors.

As for personal utensils, to get the food to your mouth, use a spoon. A spoon can do just about everything a fork can do and is more appropriate for most of the one-pot meals you'll be making. At outdoor shops you can purchase durable plastic spoons that don't break and won't conduct heat, or you can just bring one from home. Because spoons are easily lost, it pays to be careful, bring an extra, or tie a loop to your spoon and wear it around your neck.

Repair Kit

You may not be able to count on great snow conditions or finding the perfect campsite, but you can count on your equipment breaking or wearing out. What do you do when a binding screw backs out? Limp back to the car? Of course not. Just dig into your repair kit, find a replacement, and ratchet it into place with your palm-sized posidrive screwdriver.

Lots of things can go wrong with your gear on a winter camping trip, but just about everything can be fixed with a simple repair kit. Here's what you need to bring along.

• **Sewing kit.** A couple of heavy-duty needles and a spool of heavy-duty thread or a packet of dental floss will take care of most rips in your clothing or equipment. For really tough material, bring along a small awl or hole punch—a feature on most Swiss Army knives and multitools.

• **Multitool.** These little self-contained toolboxes come in handy a hundred times during a trip. For everything from cutting nylon cord to slicing cheese, they're invaluable.

- **Utility cord.** If you need to make a splint or a stretcher, if you need a clothesline or want to lash something onto your pack, if you need a new bootlace or need to lash a broken snowshoe frame, you can do it with utility cord. Bring 50 feet or so.

- **Phillips-head screwdriver.** A #3 Phillips-head fits most cross-country ski bindings. Many specialty shops sell small, palm-sized posidrive models with heads of various sizes.

- **Extra screws.** Bring extra binding screws. Oversized screws can hold a binding in place even if the original screw hole has been stripped. An assortment of screws of various sizes for general repairs is useful.

- **Pole patch kit.** If your pole breaks, you can fix it by splinting it with a pair of curved-backed snow tent stakes and duct tape. Similarly, aluminum flashing or sheet metal and hose clamps will do the job. Bring along an extra pole basket too.

- **Duct tape.** The lowly roll of duct tape is perhaps the most useful item in your repair kit. You can use it to fix just about anything: It can splint a broken pole or broken bone or patch a rip in your tent fly or shell pants. The stuff is a miracle.

- **Spare stove parts.** Bring along spare parts to fix your stove in case of breakdown.

- **Fire-starting kit.** Have a waterproof container of matches and fire-starting material hidden away in your repair kit or some other place that's dry. For fire starter, some people use solid fuel pellets or flammable liquid fire starter in tubes.

- **Vise grip.** A small vise grip comes in handy as a clamp, for loosening tight parts, as a pot grip, and for a dozen other uses.

- **Glue or epoxy.** Superglue can fix a stripped binding, broken glasses frames, and a hundred other items. Make sure to pack it carefully so it doesn't leak.

Ax and Saw

An ax and a saw are controversial equipment items, but they're indispensable to many winter travelers. With a saw and an ax, in a short time you can provide enough firewood to keep a camp warm all night, even in wet weather—an important safety consideration. And on an extended tour it's impossible to dry wet clothing, equipment, or people without a source of heat.

Without a heat source you must rely on your body to generate warmth and your clothing to retain it. With a fire, you have a powerful external heat source that can make your trip much more pleasant or can warm you in the event of serious trouble. On a cold night, a warm fire means you won't have to retire to the insulating folds of your sleeping bag as soon as you stop moving; an evening around the fire is one of the timeless reasons for taking to the winter woods in the first place.

The problem with fires in heavily used areas is obvious. Most people opposed to campfires are rightly concerned with local environmental impact and suggest the use of stoves instead. Unfortunately, stoves don't provide adequate heat output to serve as drying or warming mechanisms, and they certainly do have an impact on the environment, though not necessarily a local one.

As Garrett Conover points out, stoves have a displaced impact. "A stove user," he says, "has enlisted a global army of extractors, refiners, smelters, manufacturers, and distributors, all of whom deal with nonrenewable resources, contribute to toxic waste through manufacturing and transportation processes, and provide an end product that requires the use of finite fuels once the stoves are in use. Stoves have their place, but they are anything but a low-impact piece of equipment."

Used wisely, a lightweight ax and folding saw can make clean and efficient use of a local renewable resource—wood—and provide you with many hours of pleasure and comfort as you bask in the warmth of a fire on a cold winter night.

Wax Kit

If you're going to be skiing and you don't have waxless skis, you may choose to bring a simple wax kit. Few backcountry skiers are concerned with performance waxing—the mixing and blending and secret incantations used by nordic ski racers—but they are interested in adequate grip and glide. Many ski campers simply carry a cork, scraper, and a basic two-wax system.

The two-wax systems marketed by the major wax companies are

simple: One wax is for dry snow, the other for wet. That's it. The two canisters are color coded, red for wet and blue for dry, so you won't be confused, and that's about as complicated as it gets. Use the waxes sparingly at first, from about a foot in front of the toe binding to a foot behind the heel binding. If you need more grip, apply a thicker and longer coating. Rubbing in the wax with a cork makes it stick to the ski base longer. The beauty of the two-wax system is that it handles a wide range of snow conditions—and it performs pretty well in transition snow.

Other backcountry skiers take a full range of waxes, klisters, and wax removers. You'll definitely get better performance when you fine-tune waxes to conditions, but balance out the desire for results with the realities of skiing with packs or sleds. A compromise plan used by most backcountry skiers is to bring the two-wax system and climbing skins.

Two-way Radios

It's a layover day in camp, and half of your group wants to ski tour in the lowlands while the other wants to cut some powder turns up in the bowl. What's the easiest way for the powder hounds to inform those who want

Two-way radios are handy whenever you need to communicate with other members of your group.

to tour that they're headed back to camp for lunch? They'll give them a call on their two-way radios, naturally.

In recent years, electronics companies such as Motorola and others have completely reinvented the old walkie-talkie, replacing it with a new breed of compact, personal radios made for outdoor travelers and recreationalists. These handy devices not only add a large measure of safety by keeping separate groups in touch with each other, but they also add to the fun.

Modern two-way radios are inexpensive, powerful, and portable, and they have maximum ranges measured in miles. Two-way radios are far superior to cell phones as communications devices in the outdoors because they operate anywhere—there's no need to worry about coverage or service fees—and they generally have excellent sound quality.

Other Equipment

Naturally, every group that goes into the winter wilderness needs a first aid kit, and a suggested list of what it ought to contain is presented in appendix 2. Some items, such as sunscreen and lip balm, should be kept handy because they'll receive a lot of use.

Group Gear

Group equipment includes the following.

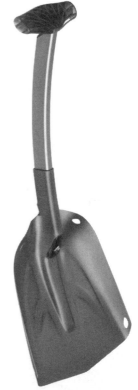

- **Shovels.** These are used for digging fire pits, building snow shelters, constructing kitchen areas, and uncovering avalanche victims if necessary. If your itinerary involves going into avalanche country, every group member should carry a shovel with a strong, tempered aluminum blade for quickly cutting through packed ice and snow.

- **Snow saws.** These are invaluable for building snow shelters and digging into wind slab or rain-hardened snow. The blades are lightweight yet sturdy aluminum with forward-canted teeth for ripping through packed snow.

All group members should carry a shovel for use in camp and as a crucial piece of avalanche safety equipment. *Photograph courtesy of Black Diamond Equipment Ltd.*

- **Rope.** A small diameter rope is helpful for added protection and support when crossing streams or descending steep or icy pitches. Adequate for most situations where a safety rope is required are 120 feet of 7- or 8-millimeter rope.

Personal Gear

Handy personal items include sunglasses for bright days and goggles for when the snow flies; a headlamp, which keeps your hands free and can be invaluable if you have to travel after dark; and an avalanche beacon and an avalanche probe, which, along with an avalanche shovel, are required when you travel in areas where slides are common. Other useful and important personal items include the following.

- **Avalung.** This nifty device manufactured by Black Diamond Equipment draws air out of the snowpack and allows you to breathe even if an avalanche buries you. Several ski mountaineers owe their lives to this crucial piece of equipment. You should carry one whenever you travel in mountainous terrain.

- **Whistle.** Attached to a tab on the shoulder strap of your pack, a whistle can be very useful when you need to get someone's attention quickly.

An Avalung can save your life if you're buried in an avalanche. *Photograph courtesy of Black Diamond Equipment Ltd.*

- **Butane lighter.** Worn on a cord around your neck to keep it warm, a butane lighter means you'll always have the means to make an emergency fire.

- **Ice ax and crampons.** These are essential for anyone planning alpine routes.

- **Compass.** Of course, everyone should have one of these and should know how to use it.

Summary Gear Checklist

Personal Gear

- ❑ Avalanche beacon
- ❑ Avalanche probe
- ❑ Avalung
- ❑ Camera/lenses/film/ extra batteries
- ❑ Compass
- ❑ Crampons
- ❑ Daypack
- ❑ Goggles
- ❑ Headlamp
- ❑ Ice ax
- ❑ Journal
- ❑ Lighter
- ❑ Pack: external or internal frame
- ❑ Reading material
- ❑ Shorty pad
- ❑ Sleeping bag
- ❑ Sleeping bag cover
- ❑ Sleeping pad
- ❑ Space blanket
- ❑ Sunglasses
- ❑ Two-way radio
- ❑ Whistle
- ❑ Wide-mouth water bottle

Group Gear

- ❑ Ax
- ❑ Bowls
- ❑ Candle lantern

❏ Coleman lantern	❏ Metal tray or lid for fire building
❏ Cooking equipment:	❏ River rescue throw rope
❏ 2 pots with lids	❏ Small-diameter rope
❏ 1 frying pan	❏ Small metal tray or license plate for stove
❏ spatula	
❏ pot grips	❏ Snow saw
❏ fireplace gloves	❏ Snow shovels
❏ reflector oven	❏ Spoons
❏ small grill	❏ Tents
❏ Cooking stove	❏ Tent stove
❏ First aid kit	❏ Towing sleds or toboggans
❏ Folding camp saw	❏ Wax kit
❏ Fuel bottles	
❏ Insulated mugs	
❏ Maps	

Chapter 6

Gear for Wearing

"This is about as wild as it gets," I thought as I gave up the lead and let someone else break trail for a while. As he passed, Stu shouted something like "What a day!" I just shook my head. No use talking—the wind whipped the words right off your lips and cast them into the great beyond.

I fell in behind Stu, second in a line of five heading down an endless white wind tunnel of a lake in northern Maine. Soon I was mesmerized by the lift and step, lift and step of his snowshoes. Flying snow pellets struck my goggles like BB shot. The wind carved the snow into delicate, enchanting shapes—little mesas, canyons, and spires—each crystal catching the sunlight like the facet of a diamond.

At noon the temperature reached a high of about –20 degrees. The wind was gusting at 40 to 50 miles per hour, hurtling across the lake like a semitruck screaming down a long grade. This deafening roar made communication impossible. We were isolated, cut off from each other. As long as we could keep moving briskly, though, as long as we had no equipment problems, as long as we didn't have to stop for very long, it was safe to keep going.

Because I was properly dressed, I wasn't conscious of being cold. I wore a few light, insulating layers under my wind parka and wind pants—a layer of synthetic long underwear, a light wool shirt and wool pants—and was thus able to stay comfortably warm while moving and to keep out the wind. On my head I wore a thin, synthetic balaclava, a hat, a face mask, goggles, and my parka hood. My feet were snug inside a layering of liner socks, two pairs of medium-weight wool socks, and mukluks. My hands were cocooned inside a warm layering of liner gloves; heavy, wool mittens; and windproof mitten shells. Not an inch of skin was exposed.

The layering worked. Each of us stayed warm and dry. We had correctly gauged the weather and our efforts. Each of us kept out the wind and kept in just enough body heat to make us comfortable. That night in camp, after all the work was done and the temperature plummeted to new depths, out came the heavy insulating layers.

Away from the fire, out on the lake at –35 degrees, I watched the stars dance in the frigid sky. I heard the trees crack and pop in the cold and listened to the lake ice boom as it contracted and shifted. Bundled up in all my layers, I felt like Neil Armstrong on the moon, but I was warm.

The key to putting together a winter camping wardrobe is to make an assessment of the weather conditions, determine your activities, and dress accordingly. Knowing that you'll be snowshoeing or skiing and pulling sleds all day, burning up about 4,000 or 5,000 calories, you sure won't need to look like the Michelin Man. The synthetic pile pullover, the heavy vest, and the parka can stay in the sled. They can come out when you stop moving, when you need them to retain body heat with heavy insulation.

On the trail, the trick is to stay warm and comfortable without overheating. Light, loose layers allow you to release most of the body heat you generate. Yet these layers trap enough warm air to keep you comfortable while keeping you from breaking a dangerous sweat, which not only robs body heat, but also reduces the insulation value of clothing by up to 90 percent. The windproof garments keep the wind from stealing too much precious warmth, yet are loose enough to allow excess heat to escape.

Layering Principles

When winter camping, wearing the right clothing combination will add to your enjoyment and performance. The key to your comfort is the layering system.

Clothing doesn't provide you with heat; your body does that. Rather, clothing provides insulation to trap your body heat, much as a thermos bottle provides insulation to keep a drink warm. Clothing insulates by trapping air between fabric fibers or layers. These spaces hold air that's been warmed by your own body heat. The more dead air space you provide, the warmer you'll be. This is why several layers of clothing are warmer than one thick layer.

Your layers must be dry in order to be effective, however. Water fills and collapses dead air space, rendering the garments virtually useless. Yet there are materials that perform better than others when damp. Wool retains some dead air space when wet, allowing you to retain some heat.

Synthetic fabrics such as pile, polypropylene, and others are very effective at heat retention when wet. Cotton, by contrast, unless it's treated or woven very finely, absorbs water and actually causes you to lose body heat through conduction.

A layering system can be broken down into three categories: inner layers, insulation layers, and outer layers.

Inner Layers

These are worn next to the skin. Inner layers provide some insulation and transfer moisture away from your skin, keeping you both warm and dry. Wool or synthetic long underwear such as polypropylene, a thin balaclava, and liner socks and gloves compose this layer.

Insulation Layers

These middle layers provide lots of dead air space that traps and retains body heat to keep you warm. Wool or synthetic pile shirts and pants, a synthetic jacket or wool sweater, and a synthetic or wool hat and mittens are standard insulating garments. In the evening you can add a heavily insulated down or synthetic parka with a hood to wear over the other layers.

Outer Layers

These act as a barrier to prevent wind and snow from stealing your warmth. Outer layers keep in your body heat and keep out inclement weather. Mitten shells, a face mask, and a shell parka and pants of waterproof, breathable fabric do the job. Be sure the shell jacket has a hood.

The layering system allows you to adjust your insulation as you heat up or cool down. Remember, you, not your clothing, are providing the warmth. So when you're snowshoeing or skiing and you start to warm up, shed a layer. If you're still too hot, take off another. Then, when you stop for lunch and are no longer cranking out the BTUs, put on all those layers again before you cool down so that you can trap a reservoir of warm air.

Each layer performs a specific, unique function. No one layer can do it all, but when you coordinate the different layers and use them properly, you'll discover how they complement each other. The result is a flexible system that can be adjusted instantly according to your needs and preference.

That's the beauty of the layer system. Now let's take a look at the various clothing components, from head to toe.

When you stop to rest or eat lunch on the trail, be sure to add layers for warmth—
and don't forget the tiara!

Clothing for the Head

The old saying about putting on a hat if your feet are cold holds true. Some 70 percent of your body heat can be lost above your shoulders. So keep your head covered, and don't neglect your neck. To reduce heat loss from the head and neck area, the best protection is a balaclava. This headpiece covers everything from your topknot to your shoulder blades while leaving an opening for your nose, eyes, and mouth.

You'll also want to bring along a hat, maybe two. At least one of these should be a thick, warm, wool or synthetic pile hat that will keep you cozy on cold days. If you wear your hat over a thin balaclava, you'll be comfortable even on bitterly cold days. The other hat can be a lightweight wool cap or a baseball cap for days when it's too warm for a heavy-duty hat or when you want to shade your face from the sun.

If you anticipate crossing exposed areas, such as mountain ridges or frozen lakes where the windchill can be severe, bring along a face mask. If they're exposed on extremely cold and windy days, your nose and cheeks can freeze quickly. On such days, ski goggles should be worn over the mask so that every inch of your skin is covered from the chilling blasts.

Clothing for the Upper Body

Keeping your core warm will go a long way toward keeping your whole body comfortable. As with your head, if your torso is well insulated, your body can afford to send blood out to your extremities to keep them warm too.

Your inner layer of long underwear should be wool or a synthetic such as polypropylene. Both materials do an excellent job of keeping your skin dry by wicking away moisture. Most winter campers choose synthetics over wool because they believe they wick better and dry faster and are more comfortable. I've used wool long underwear on my most recent trips, however, and find it similar to the synthetics in terms of performance and equally if not more comfortable to wear.

For insulation up top, bring several layers. A lightweight wool or synthetic shirt is fine for most days, but a synthetic pile jacket will be a real pleasure to throw on when you take a break or travel on really cold days. Like wool, synthetic pile retains warmth when wet. Pile is also lightweight and dries quickly. Another nice feature of pile is its warm, comfortable feel.

The latest generation of windproof and waterproof soft-shell clothing is both weatherproof and comfortable.

Bring a heavy down or synthetic fiberfill parka for stops along the trail on cold days and for cold nights. It should have a heavily insulated hood. In very cold weather you can bundle up in the parka and stand around the fire looking like the Goodyear blimp. So be it. The more you add to your girth, the warmer you'll be. As for materials, down is lightweight and easily compressed, but loses loft more readily when wet. Synthetic parkas are bulkier and heavier, but retain warmth when wet and are quick to dry.

Your outer layers must keep out the elements, so it's a good idea to bring a waterproof shell. Here again, however, you run into the problem of perspiration. If your shell doesn't breathe, then the moisture produced by your body will be trapped between layers.

Waterproof, breathable shells help transfer moisture to the outside, are reasonably waterproof, and are excellent at cutting the wind. Still, there is no way that any garment is capable of letting all your perspiration pass through if you're working hard. Even with a waterproof, breathable shell, you'll become damp from your own perspiration if you don't pace yourself and ventilate properly by keeping zippers open and sleeves open at the cuffs and leaving the shell loose at the waist. To keep perspiration to a minimum, slow your pace or stop and cool down. To retain warmth, however, do just the opposite: Cinch your garment at the waist to trap body warmth and move briskly.

Clothing for the Lower Body

Layering applies to your legs as well. Start with a layer of long underwear or synthetic tights. On a warm day when you're active, simply wear a pair of shell pants over this layer and be on your way. On a really warm day, take off the shell pants and ski in only your tights. On a cold day or in camp, add a pair of pile or fleece pants.

For your lower legs, gaiters or elastic ankle cuffs on your shell pants prevent deep snow from entering your boot tops. Many winter campers choose knee-length gaiters with Velcro flaps that cover the zippers to keep them from icing up. Shell pants designed for backcountry skiers have elastic cuffs that grip around ski boots to keep out the snow. These pants should also have

A well-dressed winter camper equipped with hard-shell jacket and pants, adjustable poles, and state-of-the-art telemark ski gear.

edge-guard patches on the inside of the ankle to keep them from being sliced by sharp ski edges. Mukluk users will not need to worry about gaiters because mukluk uppers reach to just below the knees.

Clothing for the Feet

Your feet are without doubt the toughest part of your body to keep warm and dry. They are farthest from the blood source, being at the extreme end of the body, and they are always in contact with the cold snow. In addition, they produce lots of perspiration while you ski or snowshoe, which makes it extra hard to keep them warm.

If you wear traditional, insulated winter pac boots with leather uppers and rubber bottoms, keeping your socks dry can be a real problem. Moisture from the snow permeates your boots and eventually dampens your socks. Though you can seal your boots to keep out moisture, the snow seal blocks the transfer of moisture from your feet to the outside air. If you don't block moisture from your feet right at the source, you will thoroughly soak your socks and boots from the inside. What can you do?

Fortunately, there is an answer. First, consider switching from pacs to either modern plastic ski boots or mountaineering boots with removable thermo-fit liners, or else try wearing mukluks (more on these footwear options later). Second, combine the layering system with the vapor-barrier system: Wear a thin liner sock right next to the foot. Over this wear a vapor-barrier sock—a coated nylon sock or even a thick plastic bag—to trap the moisture generated by your foot. Over the vapor barrier sock wear your heavier wool or synthetic sock. With the vapor barrier trapping foot perspiration, your insulating sock and the inside of your boot will stay dry. Some people also use foot powder or rub their feet with antiperspirant to cut down on moisture.

When you get to camp, change your damp socks to dry ones and exchange your heavy boots for a pair of cozy down or fiberfill booties. Put a felt insole inside for extra warmth, and enjoy the evening in warmth and comfort.

Clothing for the Hands

Layering for your hands begins with a pair of thin liner gloves made of silk, wool, or synthetic fiber. Liner gloves are sometimes all you need to wear on warm days or days when you're working hard and there's no wind. They keep your hands warm and dry while permitting the manual dexterity to perform tasks such as using a camera, waxing a ski, putting up a tent, and lighting a stove.

On cold days, wear wool or synthetic pile gloves over the liner gloves for more warmth. On very cold days, wear a pair of heavy mittens and cover these with mitten shells to keep out wind and water. As a last resort for cold hands or if you constantly need to remove your hands from your mittens on cold days, use chemical heat packs inside your mittens. They put out lots of heat and last for hours.

Snow School

How many snowstorms strike the continental United States each year?

An average of 105 snow-producing storms wallop the continental United States each year. •

Clothing Features

• **Size.** Your parka and shell gear will need to fit over a number of layers. The best way to be sure a shell will fit when you're purchasing it is to try it on over all the layers you plan to wear on your trip.

Other clothing items should generally fit loosely and comfortably. Tight clothing restricts your freedom of movement and reduces the amount of dead air space available between the layers.

• **Seams.** If the garment is designed to keep out water, make sure the seams are properly sealed. Most garments are sealed at the factory, but if yours isn't, do it before you head out the door. Most camping-supply stores sell tubes of seam sealer.

• **Snaps.** Avoid pieces of clothing that close only with snaps. Snaps can fill with ice and snow and then either will not close or will freeze shut. Zippers with Velcro draft flaps are preferable.

• **Zippers.** Each zipper on every piece of clothing or equipment should have a zipper pull: a piece of fabric or string that allows you to grab hold of the zipper while you're wearing mittens. Having to take your mittens off every time you need to adjust an article of clothing is a good way to get frostbitten hands.

• **Pockets.** Choose a shell garment with a couple of large pockets. You'll constantly be using them for various items such as snacks, a map, a compass, and so forth. Hand-warmer pockets are great too.

Summary Checklist of Gear for Wearing

Head	Lower Body
❏ Synthetic balaclava	❏ Synthetic or wool long underwear or tights
❏ Fleece or wool hat	
❏ Fleece neck warmer	❏ Synthetic or lightweight wool pants
❏ Face mask	❏ Waterproof, windproof shell pants
❏ Goggles	

Upper Body	Feet
❏ Synthetic or wool long underwear	❏ Synthetic or wool liner socks
❏ Lightweight synthetic or wool shirt	❏ Vapor-barrier socks (for leather pac boots)
❏ Fleece vest	❏ Synthetic or wool socks
❏ Fleece jacket	❏ Ski boots or mukluks
❏ Down or synthetic fiberfill parka	**Hands**
❏ Waterproof, windproof shell	❏ Synthetic or wool liner gloves
	❏ Synthetic or wool gloves or mittens
	❏ Waterproof, windproof mitten shells

Chapter 7

Gear for Travel

Ski designs have come a long way since the 13th century, when Norwegian king Sverre's *birkebeiner* ("birch leg," for the birch-bark leggings they wore) scouts slipped through the snowy Scandinavian forest on 8- to 12-foot-long hand-hewn boards. It wasn't until the mid-1800s, however, that Sondre Norheim, a skier from the Telemark region of Norway, took a critical look at what the birkebeiners were using and decided he could make a few improvements. By whittling a bit here and shaping a bit there, Norheim created the first pair of what we might recognize as modern skis.

Then Norheim went one step further: He attached twisted vines to the boards, wrapping them over his toes and around his heels, thus creating the first heel binding. Now Norheim not only had relatively lightweight gear, but his new bindings also allowed him to control his direction as he scampered over the landscape and down the slopes.

Soon, Norheim and his fellow Telemarkers were dominating ski competitions throughout the country. The technique they used to steer their skis—dropping into a crouch, one ski forward, one ski back—became known as the telemark turn. Ever since, backcountry skiers have been imitating Norheim and his merry men.

Leave it to another Norwegian to take Norheim's invention and put it to use on an extended trip: In 1888, Fridtjof Nansen used skis on his daring crossing of the Greenland icecap. Then, in 1911, yet another Norwegian, Roald Amundsen, used skis to become the first man at the South Pole. There was no longer any question about the usefulness of skis (by now called Norwegian snowshoes) in the winter wilderness.

Before the first ski lift was installed in 1934 in Woodstock, Vermont, skis—and skiers—were equally adept at going uphill and downhill and even jumping. When lift-served skiing eliminated the need to climb, however, the sport became much more specialized. The backcountry skier, with his do-it-all equipment, was almost eclipsed by the flashy alpine skier, with his shiny outfits and locked-down heels.

That didn't happen, though, and today telemark is the fastest growing segment of the ski industry.

Telemark Skis

For many winter campers, telemark skis are the ultimate form of backcountry transportation because they let you travel swiftly on the flats, they climb well, and they're a lot of fun on the downhills. These days, telemark skis are virtually indistinguishable from alpine skis, but there are some subtle differences: Telemark skis are typically a little lighter than alpine skis, and they tend to have a slightly softer flex, which means it takes less pressure to bend them into an arc.

Here are some things to look for in a telemark ski.

Flex. If you anticipate skiing a lot of fluffy powder, look for a pair of skis with soft flex to help you navigate the deep, unconsolidated snow frequently found in the backcountry. A softer flex will let the ski tip rise above the soft snow, whereas a stiffer flex will tend to bury the tip. If you'll be spending spend a lot of time skiing more mixed conditions, look for a ski with medium flex to handle a wider variety of snow conditions.

Length. The correct ski length depends on several factors, such as your weight, your skiing ability, and the ski model itself. If you plan to spend the majority of your time on steep slopes or if you like to ski fast, a slightly longer ski will be more stable and will provide more control. Shorter skis are easier to maneuver in variable terrain and where there are tight trees, because

Today's telemark skis are short, wide, and shapely. *Photograph courtesy of Black Diamond Equipment Ltd.*

they generally turn more quickly than longer skis. When you're buying skis, check the manufacturer's suggested sizing, but also ask a knowledgeable and experienced sales associate for more information.

Width. These days, most telemark skis are generally as wide as alpine skis, which means they're wide enough for floating through backcountry snow while supporting both your weight and the added weight of your pack. Yet you should still choose a ski with a width that matches the terrain where you plan to ski.

A ski with a narrow waist lets you transfer your weight from one edge of the ski to the other edge more quickly than a ski with a wide waist. This quick edge-to-edge capability makes it a faster-turning ski. In addition, with a narrow-waist ski, you spend more time on your edges, which gives you more control in hardpack or icy conditions. Unfortunately, the narrow waist means these skis are not what you'll need when the snow gets soft and deep. For powder conditions, you'll need a wide ski to float through all that ephemeral fluff.

Sidecut. Sidecut is the parabolic, or hourglass, shape of the ski that makes it easy to turn. Basically, sidecut is the difference between the width of the ski's waist and its tip and tail. Most modern telemark skis have waists that are anywhere from 25 to 40 millimeters narrower than their tips and tails. The wide tips let the skis float through powder and plow through mixed backcountry snow, while the accentuated curve of the narrower waists allow them to carve turns much more easily than the old straight skis.

Camber. Unlike the telemark skis of yore with their double camber, today's modern telemark skis have single, or alpine, camber, which means there's very little arch from tip to tail. Unlike the old skis with their raised wax pockets underfoot, telemark skis with alpine camber distribute your weight evenly over the full length of the ski, which allows for smooth, continuous edging while you turn.

Telemark Ski Boots

Black Diamond and Scarpa began the plastic telemark boot revolution in 1992 with the introduction of the Terminator, and leather boots instantly became ancient history. Scarpa's all-plastic buckle boot lived up to its name (terminating leather boots for all time) and delivered the goods by providing more power and control to telemark skiers of all abilities.

Modern plastic telemark boots

Garmont and Crispi quickly followed suit, and today all three manufacturers offer warm, lightweight, low-maintenance, powerful, and durable plastic telemark boots with thermo-moldable custom liners.

As with telemark skis, there's a telemark boot for nearly every situation. For backcountry skiers who will spend most of their time on the flats or low-angle slopes, there are lightweight, touring-oriented telemark boots with low cuffs and two buckles. For skiers who plan to spend most of their time making steep descents, there are heavy, high-cuff, four-buckle boots offering the maximum in power and control.

Most backcountry skiers don't want or need either a very light or very heavy telemark boot. If the boot is too light, it won't allow you to put the necessary power into today's bigger skis. Because backcountry telemarkers are skinning up as much as they're skiing down, they generally don't want to carry big, heavy boots either.

Most backcountry telemarkers choose a boot that falls between the superlight and superheavy boots. These have three buckles and moderately high cuffs and are made of stiffer plastic than touring boots. The trade-off is that though they do everything well, they lack the power, weight, and stiffness of the super-high-performance boots.

Which boot you chose for your trip depends upon where you're going and what you hope to accomplish once you're there. If your objective is primarily to ski downhill, you may decide to sacrifice weight for added control. In that case, the large, four-buckle boots, with their substantially higher cuffs and much stiffer plastic construction, make the most sense.

When selecting boots, make certain to focus on comfort. Backcountry skiing involves a lot of uphill travel, which can be hard on your feet. Choose a boot with adequate toe room and little or no heel lift.

Telemark Bindings

Telemark bindings have come a long way in recent years, and the venerable three-pin nordic binding is truly a thing of the past. Today's telemark bindings are heavier, larger, more durable, and much more expensive than their predecessors. Despite the cost, they do an excellent job of keeping boots and skis connected while holding up to the severe abusive stresses telemarkers put on them with their constant edging, twisting, and turning.

Most backcountry telemark skiers choose cable bindings with compression-spring cartridges. Their beefy construction makes them the best choice for use with modern, heavy plastic telemark boots.

Some of the newer bindings feature free-hinging toe pieces when they're set in touring mode. The resistance-free pivot feels more like an alpine touring binding as you climb, and it saves a lot of energy when you're skinning up.

In the last several years binding manufacturers have started to introduce releasable telemark bindings. If your travel plan includes backcountry skiing in potential avalanche terrain, you might consider a releasable binding. If your skis stay attached to your feet in a slide, they might pull you down in the snow. Also, some telemarkers choose releasable bindings because they feel they might reduce the risk of knee injury during a fall.

Some telemark bindings have a free-hinging toe piece that makes skinning up much easier.
Photograph courtesy of Black Diamond Equipment Ltd.

Alpine Touring Skis

Alpine touring skis are also called ski mountaineering or randonee skis. (*Randonee* is a French word for "touring in the mountains," although free-heel skiers insist it actually means "can't telemark." Randonee skiers retort that *telemark* is actually Norwegian for "slow hippie.")

As technology and equipment continue to evolve, the differences between alpine, telemark, and alpine touring skis continue to blur. These days, many telemarkers use alpine touring skis, while an equal number of randonee skiers choose telemark skis. There just isn't that much difference anymore.

Alpine Touring Ski Boots

Alpine touring boots look very similar to both alpine ski boots and plastic mountaineering boots, but unlike alpine ski boots, alpine touring boots come with rubber lug soles for traction that rocks underfoot to make hiking easier. Another difference is that the upper cuffs on alpine touring boots can be unlocked for greater comfort and flexibility while skinning or hiking.

As with telemark boots, alpine touring boots come in different models made for different purposes. They range from low-top touring boots to high-performance, high-top, four-buckle monsters that are perfect for the steep and deep.

Remember that when choosing alpine touring boots, it's important to make sure they're compatible with your alpine touring bindings.

Alpine Touring Bindings

Unlike alpine ski bindings that offer only one position—a locked-down heel—alpine touring bindings feature two positions: one with the heel free and the toe pivoting on a hinge for striding and climbing and another one with the heel locked down for parallel skiing. Alpine touring bindings include multiposition heel lifters to take the strain off your lower legs during a steep ascent.

As with alpine ski bindings, most alpine touring bindings are step-in—that is, they lock the heel when you insert your foot. The bindings unlock

Alpine touring bindings are free at the heel for traveling uphill or on the flats, and they can be locked down for descent. *Photograph courtesy of Black Diamond Equipment Ltd.*

with a push of your ski pole, and they release at the toe and the heel when you take a forceful fall. As with alpine ski bindings, you can set the Deutsches Institut für Normungon (known as the DIN—an international standard scale) on alpine touring bindings so they release only when you want them to.

Telemark or Alpine Touring?

Deciding between telemark and alpine touring gear depends upon your previous experience and which kind of ski technique you prefer to use. If you're already an alpine skier but haven't learned to telemark, using alpine touring equipment will allow you to ski in the backcountry using an already familiar technique, whereas purchasing telemark gear will require that you learn a whole new skill. Either way will get you up and down the mountains.

Snowboards

Today's split boards combine the rush of riding a surfboard with the ease of climbing a mountain on telemark skis. The bad old days when back-country snowboarders (riders) had to walk in on snowshoes while packing their snowboards are long gone. With a split board, all a backcountry rider needs is the board, boots, collapsible poles, and climbing skins.

Split boards detach from tip to tail down the center and essentially form two short cross-country skis. When the rider attaches climbing skins to the base of each half of the board, he or she can ascend mountains just like a skier. At the summit the rider removes the climbing skins, recon-

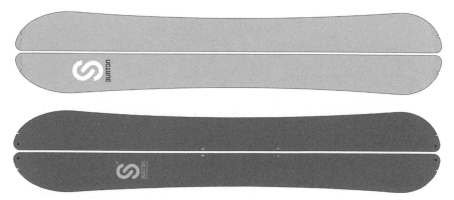

A split board easily converts to two "skis" for climbing. *Photograph © Burton Snowboards.*

nects the two halves of the board to form a snowboard, and enjoys the ride down. This transition requires minimal tools and takes only a couple of minutes.

Most split boards are designated as freeride or all-mountain boards. These split boards are relatively long and relatively narrow with a deeper sidecut than regular snowboards. Freeride split boards are the tools of choice for backcountry riders because they offer a smooth, stable, responsive, and predictable ride, and they perform well in the entire gamut of backcountry snow conditions, including powder, ice, crud, and crust.

Snowboard Boots

As with telemark and alpine touring boots, choosing the right pair of snowboard boots can mean the difference between suffering excruciating pain or enjoying perfect comfort on your backcountry tour. Spend the necessary time to find a pair that fits well, is designed for your riding style, and is matched with your binding system. There are basically two types of snowboarding boots.

• **Soft boots.** These boots feature a flexible outer boot, a padded liner, and a treaded sole for grip and traction. Many riders prefer soft boots simply for their comfortable fit.

• **Hard boots.** Hard boots look very similar to alpine ski boots, but as with alpine touring boots, they have lateral mobility at the ankle. Hard boots feature a plastic outer shell, a treaded sole for grip and traction, and a thick padded liner. They're usually adjusted with buckles and clips. Many backcountry riders choose hard boots for their increased ankle support and the added control they provide on the downhill run.

Snowboard Bindings

When split boards are divided, the two halves become skis, which means the bindings must adapt to this new form of self-propulsion. Fortunately, split boards come with mounting hardware that allows the bindings to be placed facing forward on each ski, just like cross-country ski bindings. Each of these bindings is attached to the split board only at the toe when the board is in ski mode. The heel is free so the rider can skin up the mountain just like a telemarker or someone who's alpine touring. There are three basic types of bindings.

- **Strap bindings.** These are the most common bindings and are used by riders who prefer soft boots. They generally feature two adjustable ratchet straps and multiple adjustment options for strap positioning.
- **Step-in bindings.** These bindings easily fasten the boot to the board without straps. Step-in bindings are boot specific, so you'll need to buy boots and bindings together as a system. Choose your boots first, and then get a compatible step-in binding.
- **Plate bindings.** These bindings feature a hard base plate, steel bails, and a heel lever. Plate bindings are used in combination with hard boots that are inserted into the toe and heel pieces, just as with a ski. By flipping up the heel lever, the boots are locked into the bindings. To step out of the binding, simply flip down the heel lever. Plate bindings most resemble ski bindings, and their tough construction and rigid responsiveness provide maximum control and power for high-speed carving and riding in tough snow conditions.

Poles

Two-piece, lightweight adjustable poles can make backcountry skiing much more enjoyable because they can be shortened for skiing downhill and lengthened for climbing. Certain models can also be linked together to form avalanche probes, although you should always bring a true avalanche probe with you regardless of this feature.

It is well worth spending a little extra to purchase the lightest poles you can find. New carbon fiber models have drastically cut the swing weight of the best modern ski poles, which means it's a lot easier to keep your hands up and in front of you, where they belong when you ski downhill, resulting in an overall better skiing stance.

An avalanche probe. *Photograph courtesy of Black Diamond Equipment Ltd.*

A lightweight, adjustable-length carbon fiber pole *Photograph courtesy of Black Diamond Equipment Ltd.*

Climbing Skins

In the old days, climbing skins were just that: ski-length strips of animal hide that skiers attached to the bottom of their skis. With the hairs pointing toward the tail of the ski, the skins gave the skis a tenacious grip on steep uphills when the skier pressed down. At the top, the skiers simply ripped the hides from the bottoms of their skis, and continued on their way.

Today, climbing skins are made of synthetic fibers, but they perform the same function as the original hides: As the ski glides forward, the hairs provide little resistance. If the ski starts to slip backward, however, the hairs dig into the snow and hold.

Without skins, many routes commonly enjoyed by backcountry skiers and split-board riders would be inaccessible. Skins are essential to climbing any trail that is more than moderately steep.

Miscellaneous Skiing Items

• **Knee pads.** When you're five days from medical help, the best medicine is prevention, and the easiest way to avoid smashing a kneecap on a buried rock or stump is to wear a pair of telemark kneepads. When you ski the backcountry, your knees can't avoid coming into contact with the snow, your skis, and other objects. These little insurance policies are sold in specialty ski and snowboard shops and are designed so you can put them on under your shell pants without removing your boots.

• **Ski leashes.** Leashes attach your binding to your boot. Most skiers don't use them in the backcountry, and you should never use them in avalanche terrain. When you go to a ski area to sharpen your skiing skills, however, you'll be required to use them.

• **Heel lifters.** These are sturdy metal bails that can be flipped up to raise your heels while you climb steep slopes with skins. By raising your heels, the lifters reduce lower leg fatigue, making even the steepest ascents no more strenuous on your calves than climbing a staircase.

Snowshoes

The snowshoe, like the wheel, is one of those creations that revolutionized human life. Before the first snowshoes were invented thousands of years ago, people simply couldn't live on parts of the globe that were sub-

Synthetic climbing skins attach to ski bases and make it easy to climb mountain trails.

stantially snow covered. Doing so would have meant floundering in the white stuff, making it impossible to travel, hunt, and move with the seasons or the game. *Raquettes,* as the French Canadian fur traders called snowshoes, enabled people to move around in deep snow and to move into areas previously off-limits to people on foot.

Nothing has changed in the intervening years. If you want to travel in

Snowshoes allow you to travel over the surface of deep snow.

snow country, you need a way to stay afloat on the drifts. Skis are one way to get around in the snow; snowshoes are another.

Credit the northern-forest Indians with perfecting the snowshoe. Unlike Eskimos in Alaska or the Inuit in Canada, who, for the most part, live in a landscape of hard, wind-packed snow and ice where snowshoes aren't really necessary; many Indian nations inhabit the northern forest regions of more temperate latitudes, where the winters are long and the snows pile high. For them, snowshoes are an essential means of transportation.

Snowshoes come in all sorts of shapes and sizes, but the variety of forms is not just the result of different artistic sensibilities. They're different because they're designed to perform specific functions. As with skis, the design characteristics determine the strengths and weaknesses of the various models. Before we discuss particular designs, however, let's look at general characteristics.

Snowshoe Materials

Frame materials. These haven't changed much over the years. The two widely available choices are wood and metal, each having its own advantages and disadvantages. For many snowshoers, traditional wood is still the material of choice. There are several reasons for this, including tradition, aesthetics, and feel. Wood is strong and supple, flexing under stress while providing stability and support. Wooden snowshoes are also available in a wide variety of shapes, sizes, and modifications.

For trips in mountain environments, though, metal snowshoes can't be beat. The metal frames give them incredible strength and durability. Virtually impossible to break in the field, metal snowshoes are safe and very reliable in the roughest terrain. Even when bridged between rocks while supporting the full weight of the climber and his or her gear, they will not bend or break. Also, metal snowshoes have a crampon under the ball of the foot for excellent grip while you're climbing.

Webbing. Also called lacing, filling, or decking, this is the material that's attached to the snowshoe frame to support the weight of the snowshoer over the snow.

The webbing must be made of a tough, tight, abrasion-resistant material. The pattern of the woven webbing depends upon snow conditions. The weaving of the pattern is very close for a shoe used in light, fine, frost snow and is more open for a snowshoe used in coarse or wind-packed snow.

There are a few basic types of snowshoe webbing. Babiche is the traditional choice—Indians use the hides of beaver, bear, caribou, and moose. Modern commercial babiche is usually made from steer hide. Though still popular with traditionalists, it's not foolproof: Babiche can soak up water when used in heavy, wet snow, and the laces may stretch and sag under these conditions. To prevent this from becoming a problem, the laces must be treated annually with a waterproofing varnish.

Neoprene, a rubber-coated nylon, is generally acknowledged as a superior filling because, unlike babiche, the neoprene does not soak up moisture, nor does it stretch or sag from moisture or use. Neoprene is very strong, resists decay, and lasts longer than babiche. Still, it's not perfect: Coarse snow or crust can fray the neoprene, causing snow to collect and freeze to the frayed strands, which must be clipped or burned off unless you want to end up carrying around a lot of extra weight.

On most modern snowshoes, the decking is made of either a durable, cold-resistant rubber or a plastic material. Tough, rubber decking material such as Hypalon is very flexible and lightweight. Plastic composite decking material is more rigid and is quite durable. Both of these materials are fine choices.

Snowshoe Design

Choose your snowshoes according to your needs: the terrain you'll be traveling, snow conditions, and your weight. Is your trip primarily a steep mountain route, or will you wade through the deep snows of interior forests? Will you be in heavy brush or on the snowy, wind-packed surfaces of lakes and rivers? There's a snowshoe design best suited to every type of terrain.

Snowshoe designs range from the flat, circular shoes with very fine webbing used by the Naskapi, Cree, and Montagnais Indians of Quebec and Labrador to the long, narrow snowshoes used by Gwich'in and Koyukon Indians of interior Alaska.

Key design and fit characteristics of snowshoes include these.

- **Width.** The more surface area a snowshoe has, the more flotation over the snow it provides. This is especially true when the surface is combined with fine-weave webbing. A wide snowshoe can also be short, making it more maneuverable in brush.
- **Length.** When crossing open country, where maneuverability is not a problem, long snowshoes provide equal surface area to wide shoes, and

thus approximately equal flotation. It's easier to go quickly with long shoes because they're narrow, like skis.

- **Weave.** The finer the weave (or the more solid the decking), the more the shoe will float atop the snow surface.
- **Tip.** An upturned tip will let the snowshoe tip rise clear of the depression it makes in the snow without catching. This is an especially helpful feature on steep uphills.
- **Tail.** The tails of longer snowshoes help keep the snowshoes tracking in a straight line. Also, they provide a counterweight to the tips, so that when you lift the snowshoe, the tails drag on the snow behind and the tips rise above the snow.

Types of Snowshoes

The wide, circular snowshoe used by the Naskapi, Cree, and Montagnais Indians of eastern Canada is excellent for use in areas of deep snow and heavy brush; the fine weave and extreme width keep it from sinking, while the short length makes maneuvering easy. It has a flat tip and may have a slight tail.

The Alaska shoe, a long, narrow snowshoe, is at home in the deep powder of more open country. With an overall surface area equivalent to the Naskapi shoe, the Alaska shoe floats well, but the relative narrowness of its width combined with its extreme length make this model perform more like a ski in open country. The long tail of the Alaska shoe helps it track in a straight line. The upturned tip keeps the shoe from diving into the snow with every step.

In between these extreme designs are the snowshoes commonly available in sporting goods and outdoors stores. The most popular and most versatile models incorporate characteristics of both the Naskapi and Alaskan models.

The standard bear paw. This is a relatively short, relatively wide, tailless shoe. Its features make it simple yet maneuverable. Its balance and short length preclude the need for an upturned tip and a tail. The bear paw is small and lightweight and is at home in deep snow, thick brush, and hilly terrain. Because of its versatility, the bear paw is popular with trappers and others who work in the woods.

The modified or Green Mountain bear paw is a slightly longer and slightly narrower version of the standard bear paw. Like the standard bear paw, the Green Mountain is at home in a variety of conditions and is perhaps the most popular model for general use.

The Maine or Michigan snowshoe. This is the model most people envision when they think of snowshoes. Teardrop shaped, the Maine starts out wide in front, tapers back to a tail in the rear, and has an upturned toe. The Maine is a cross between the Alaska and the bear paw and incorporates many good qualities of both. The Maine snowshoe is an excellent choice for carrying heavy loads in a wide variety of conditions.

What Size Snowshoe?

The size snowshoe you choose will depend on where you plan to travel and what types of snow conditions you expect. The area covered by your snowshoe and the closeness of the webbing weave are what provide you with flotation in deep snow. A rule of thumb is that the wider the surface area and the closer the weave, the greater the amount of flotation. So if you plan to travel in an area where cold, light snow conditions prevail, you'll need a

With its wide shape and tapered tail, the Maine snowshoe works well in many conditions.

wider, more closely woven snow-shoe than you would for a trip in hard-packed conditions.

Snowshoe manufacturers provide charts matching snowshoe size to your weight to help you choose frame size. Use these charts only as a guideline. When you select a snow-shoe, don't forget to add to your body weight to the weight you'll be carrying on your back. You may carry 50 pounds or more on a winter camping trip, so make sure to get a snowshoe that is beefy enough for the job.

Snowshoeing Footwear

Unless you do all your winter camping in the mountains, there will be times when you won't need a boot for backcountry snow-shoeing. Say you're planning to snowshoe the frozen waterways of Minnesota's Boundary Waters, for example. On flat surfaces in extremely cold conditions the best choice for footwear is a pair of mukluks. This soft, traditional Native American footwear is ideal for winter camping when a rigid boot isn't critical.

Mukluks are lightweight, one-piece moccasins that reach to just under the knee. To wear them, simply insert felt liners, put on a couple of pairs of warm socks, and lace up the boots. Mukluks are lighter than leather pac boots and are much warmer. Flexible and breathable, mukluks are a real treat for your feet; wearing them on snowshoes is like snowshoeing in a pair of toasty warm slippers. Steger Mukluks in Ely, Minnesota, makes a model with rubberized elk hide soles that work beautifully whether you're simply walking in snow or walking with snowshoes.

Snowshoe Bindings

Like a telemark ski binding, the snowshoe binding keeps your foot secured to the snowshoe while allowing your heel to lift with every step.

Snow School

Where does the word *winter* come from? *According to the Library of Congress, the word* winter *comes from a Germanic term meaning "time of water" and refers to the season's precipitation. The winter solstice, the official beginning of the season, is the time of the year when the sun is at its point farthest south of the equator.*

In the Northern Hemisphere, winter begins on the shortest day of the year, around December 21, and lasts until the vernal equinox, around March 20, which is the official beginning of spring.

Ironically, March is frequently the snowiest month of the year in some northern and mountain states. •

Traditional bindings are made of a length of cotton lamp wicking tied in a pattern called the squaw stitch around the heel and toe. The squaw stitch is a light, simple, inexpensive binding, but tying it has become something of a lost skill among the vast majority of winter campers.

Modern snowshoe bindings typically consist of a platform you step onto and nylon straps that go over the foot and around the heel, holding the foot quite snugly to the snowshoe. For travel in rugged country, especially while traversing a slope, this added support makes a big difference.

Winter campers need bindings that pivot under the balls of the feet where the binding attaches to the decking. This rotating motion allows the tails of the snowshoes to drop down as you step forward, thereby shedding snow and reducing leg fatigue. Tail drop also keeps the snowshoes tracking in a straight line in deep snow.

Snowshoe Traction Devices

Modern snowshoes come with an array of toothy devices to help you get a firm grip in steep and icy conditions.

- **Instep crampons.** These are placed beneath the binding plate, so they'll pivot with your feet and dig in as you climb.

- **Heel crampons.** These are usually located beneath the decking, where they're arrayed in a V to reduce your speed as you descend a steep slope.

- **Traction bars.** These are placed beneath the decking, parallel to your feet. They reduce side slipping as you move across steep slopes.

Summary Checklist of Travel Gear

- ❏ Telemark skis
- ❏ Alpine touring skis
- ❏ Split snowboard
- ❏ Telemark ski boots
- ❏ Alpine touring ski boots
- ❏ Snowboard boots
- ❏ Snowshoes
- ❏ Mukluks
- ❏ Poles
- ❏ Climbing skins
- ❏ Knee pads

Chapter 8

Food and Nutrition

Guides have their folk heroes too—the more colorful, the better—and Alferd Packer is many a mountain guide's hero, a man as colorful as his name is twisted. His exploits earned him everlasting fame. He even became a patron saint of the Colorado Republican Party.

The story goes that in 1873, Packer was hired to guide a hunting party in the Colorado Rockies. During a blizzard, he and five of his guests became lost and snowbound. When spring arrived, down from the mountains came Alferd, fit and well fed, none the worse for his ordeal—but his five clients were nowhere to be found. Search parties discovered the macabre remains of the five missing hunters, each showing definite signs of foul play.

Packer was arrested, of course, and charged with cannibalism, but what the judge declared when he found Packer guilty launched the demented mountaineer into immortality: "Alferd Packer," said the judge, "you voracious, man-eating son of a bitch. There were only seven Democrats in Hinsdale County, and you ate five of them!"

The annals of exploration are fraught with similar stories of privation: the Donner party caught in the wintry Sierra, Adolphus Greely and his men trapped at Fort Conger, John Hornby and Edgar Christian waiting in the frozen Barrens for the caribou that never came, the Franklin expedition hauling their silver tea sets across the ice of King William Island. They're gruesome stories—just frightful—but great for telling around the campfire while enjoying a hot meal.

Fear not. The chances are excellent that your meals won't be quite so exotic as Packer's. They will, however, be nutritious, filling, and tasty. If you think winter camping food consists of cold oatmeal, gruel, and mush, read on.

Eat up! Food Is Fuel

The importance of food on a winter camping trip can't be overstated. Food supplies you with the energy you need to travel all day and stay warm all night. When you get enough of the right foods to eat, you'll be healthy, happy, and ready to go. Good meals go a long way toward ensuring high morale and top physical performance.

You need a lot of food in the winter woods. That faceless character, the average American, consumes some 2,700 calories per day while living a sedentary life. (Incredibly, the average American spends only 10 minutes per day outside.) This is too much to eat when just sitting around—meaning the sedentary American tends to get a little chubby—but 2,700 calories per day is a starvation diet for anyone on the winter trail. If you consume too little food, you risk fatigue and hypothermia.

How many calories are required to carry a pack or pull a sled in the cold for eight or nine hours a day? You can start figuring around 4,000 calories per person per day and bump it up from there. That translates to about 2 to $2\frac{1}{2}$ pounds of food per person per day. Don't worry about eating too much, though; few people gain weight on a winter camping trip. In fact, it can be a great way to work off any excess.

Consume Variety

As a rule of thumb, 50 percent of your food intake should be in the form of carbohydrates, which give your body quick, efficient energy. Foods such as sugar or honey, rice, pasta, and cereal are excellent sources of carbohydrates.

About 20 percent of your food should be proteins, from meats, cheese, milk, grains, beans, and nuts. Proteins are important for cell maintenance and growth.

The remaining 30 percent or so (remember, individual needs vary) should be in the form of fat. Fats contain more than twice the calories per pound than either proteins or carbohydrates, making them essential, efficient foods for packing into the winter wilderness. One experienced winter explorer satisfies his body's craving for fats by munching on sticks of butter as if they were candy bars! Examples of foods that contain fat are butter and margarine, cooking oil, salami, pepperoni and sausage, cheese, nuts, and peanut butter.

Vitamins and minerals will be well represented if you plan a well-balanced diet from the foods listed above. Water-soluble vitamins—the B and C groups—can be replenished daily by bringing vitamin-fortified fruit drinks or by bringing along a supply of vitamins from home.

A word on variety: You can eat the same healthy and filling meal every day and meet your nutritional requirements, but your stomach will rebel if you don't provide it with a change now and then. Try to build in different textures, flavors, and smells when you put together your meal plan.

How meticulous do you need to be in planning for the major food groups? Not very. Basically, you can eat what you eat at home, just more of it. If you're an active person, you know what your body needs. What you must take into consideration beyond nutritional concerns, however, is the weight and the bulk of your food supplies.

The Basic Ingredients

You can look at the following list of basic ingredients and use your imagination to combine them to create your own tasty concoctions. You can either plan meals ahead of time or bring along the raw materials and get creative in the field.

Fresh foods. Avoid fresh foods for the most part. Because of their high water content they tend to be heavy and spoil quickly. Exceptions are butter and cheese, meats such as bacon or sausage, baked goods such as cookies and brownies, nuts, and meats such as salami and pepperoni. These foods take up less space than, say, fresh eggs, fruits, and vegetables, and they provide plenty of concentrated nutrition for their weight.

Dry foods. The bulk of your food should be dry—foods with 95 percent or more of the water removed. These nonperishables lighten the load and are available at most neighborhood grocery stores. They include mixed dried vegetables; dried onion, garlic, and potatoes; sunflower seeds and soybeans; egg or whole-grain pastas such as spaghetti, macaroni, and noodles; and Ramen noodle packets.

Also bring grains: rice, corn, and oatmeal (granola and other cereals make wonderful hot breakfasts if you throw in some nuts, raisins, and a spoonful of butter or margarine along with some honey or brown sugar); beans and lentils; dried milk; fruits such as raisins, peaches, and apricots; and lots of dried soup and sauce mixes for bases and added flavoring.

Also available in local markets are prepackaged dried dinners that are lightweight and easy to prepare. These meals can be fancy, with such repasts as stroganoff and fettuccini Alfredo on the menu. As with all prepackaged foods, if you believe the number of suggested servings on the box, you'll go hungry. If it says "serves eight," it might just make a meal for two hungry winter campers.

Freeze-dried foods. These meals are extremely lightweight and require only minimal preparation and cooking time. Most of them have to be merely soaked in hot water for a few minutes and—voilà!—shrimp Creole! As a longtime skeptic of these mealtime miracles, I was completely won over by freeze-dried food while on a winter traverse of New Hampshire's Presidential Range.

During the multiday crossing, we endured gales and subzero temperatures. In those extreme conditions the last thing anyone wanted to do was play Julia Child. Not only did the freeze-dried dinners weigh almost nothing, enabling us to move rapidly over the exposed mountain summits, but they were also delicious and provided excellent nutrition. The drawback to freeze-dried food is the higher price you pay for the convenience.

Extras. Don't forget the little extras to spice up your food and add some zip to your creations! Add soup, sauce mixes, and even bouillon cubes to meals for enhanced flavor. Honey, syrup, and brown sugar provide lots of calories and taste to breakfast. Sprinkle real bacon bits onto your dinners for some extra flavor and calories, and bring along some popcorn for a fun after-dinner snack.

Herbs and spices. Jazz up your meals with a small selection of herbs and spices too. Salt and pepper, cayenne, garlic and onion, cumin, chili powder, real bacon bits, and Italian seasoning weigh only an ounce or so each and can make the difference between a so-so meal and a culinary delight. Some people pack them in 35-millimeter film canisters and label them. Fuji film canisters are best because they're clear, allowing you to see what's in them before you dump the contents onto your food.

One-pot simplicity. On a winter camping trip, simplicity is best, so using one large pot for cooking makes the most sense. That way, all of the ingredients are already combined, making preparation easy, and the minimal cleanup required leaves you free to travel farther before dinner, explore around camp, or relax around the campfire and enjoy a hot drink.

Hot drinks. Keep the hot drinks coming! Another pot can be used as a hot-water supply for cocoa, coffee, and regular or herbal tea. Add a lump of butter or margarine to a hot drink for some extra energy to keep you warm. I can't conceive of not starting and ending my day with lots of hot drinks.

What about Lunch?

There are two ways—maybe more—to have lunch. One way is to begin lunch right after breakfast and keep eating until dinner. You need lots of energy on the trail, so eat plenty and often.

For munching on the trail, some people pack gorp (good old raisins and peanuts—with M&Ms tossed in, of course) in a resealable bag. Others bring along some cut-up cheese and salami or sausage sticks. (Cutting cheese or sausage in advance before they freeze is a good idea.) When everyone packs a different item, you can mix and match. If you choose this mobile method of eating lunch, make sure the foods you bring along are easily packed and are accessible.

The other way to have lunch is more relaxed: Find a place to stop that's out of the wind and in the sun and that overlooks some scenic vista. If it's cold, bundle up, start a stove, and make hot drinks. If you really want to do it right, build a small fire and relax on your sleeping pad. Take off your boots and socks and warm your toes. Dig into your pack and have a handful of gorp. Sharpen a stick and roast some sausage or pepperoni to bring out the flavor. Put a pot of water on and make tea or coffee or hot cocoa. What's the rush? This is living!

Lunch on the trail is a great time to relax. What's the rush?

Packing Efficiently

It happens every trip. It's 8 PM, cold, and dark. Everybody's hungry, and the cook is frantically trying to locate the macaroni and cheese. Soon, everyone is rooting through stuff sacks. Headlamp beams search out the lost meal supplies, and tempers flash in the night.

"I thought you had all the dinners!"

"And I thought you'd set aside everything we needed for today's meals!"

"Why don't you two shut up! We need to devise a better system so we don't go through this every night!"

Here's how to avoid this scenario: Once you've purchased the food, remove all the packaging. You can save an incredible amount of weight and bulk by stripping off all the cardboard and plastic. Better yet, purchase your food in bulk at a co-op. Repack the food in plastic bags, the kind you get at your local supermarket produce section work well and can double as vapor-barrier socks. Use double bags to make sure the food doesn't spill onto other items. Be sure to save any cooking instructions from the boxes and put them in the bags with the food. Identify what's in each bag with a bold marking pen. Remember, cornmeal, pancake mix, dried milk, and lemonade powder all look alike in the dark.

Snow School

Which mountain receives more average annual snow: Vail, Colorado, or Jay Peak, Vermont?

Jay Peak, with 355 inches to Vail's 348 inches. •

If the bags are long enough, twist the tops and tie a slipknot to seal each. Overhand knots are impossible to undo. Metal twist-ties already carpet the ground around many campsites, so it's best to keep them out of the woods.

You can save a lot of time if you mix your meals in advance and package them before you begin your trip. You can even plan when you'll eat them and mark the bag accordingly. A bag marked D-6 for instance, means "dinner, day 6."

Now what do you do with that mound of food? One way to handle it is to pack each meal in separate stuff sacks so that all the breakfasts are together, for instance, and likewise for the lunches and dinners. Pack condiments and extras in their own stuff sack. With this method, you need only find one stuff sack at mealtime. If you color code the stuff sacks—say yellow is for breakfast, red for dinner—you'll be that much more efficient. You can use as many stuff sacks as there are people in the group to distribute the weight evenly.

Another way to divvy up the food is to divide it into equal portions according to the number of people in the group. Then each evening, plan the next day's meals and put everything you'll need for the day to come—breakfast, lunch, dinner—in a separate stuff sack. This method requires daily reorganization but works just as well.

Food Caches

Setting up food caches can be a great way to lighten your load and extend your range. If you're going out for ten days to a couple of weeks or more, you need to think seriously about resupplying along the way.

Take a look at your proposed route. Are there places where you cross a road or intersect a hiking trail? Find accessible spots that are five to ten days apart and set up your caches. Drive and then hike in to the spot and set up your cache.

Make sure that your supplies are well packed and impermeable to moisture and are well concealed in rugged containers. The last thing you need is to arrive at a cache and find that someone or something has tampered with it.

Double-bag your supplies in plastic and then place them inside sealed plastic containers. Camouflage your caches well. You can hang them or cover them. Whatever you do, make sure you know where they are. Locate each cache on your maps like a buried treasure: X marks the spot! You may want to include a note in the cache addressed to anyone who might discover it, telling them what it's for and asking them not to tamper with it.

Besides food, you can stock your cache with dry socks, matches, batteries, and maps for the next section of your trip. You can even include a flask of something special. Be creative! Just be sure to return to all of your cache sites after the trip and clean up everything you've left behind.

Another ingenious way I've heard of to cache your food in really cold regions is to chip a trench in the ice of a frozen lake or river. Place your items in the trench and then fill the trench with water. The water will freeze in a matter of minutes, and your supplies will be safely sealed in the ice until you chip them out.

Food Chart

Breakfast	Lunch	Dinner	Dessert	Extras
Coffee	Pepperoni or sausage	Macaroni and cheese	Cakes	Sunflower seeds
Hot cocoa	Cheese	Spaghetti	Brownies	Nuts
Tea or herb tea	Gorp	Noodle casseroles	Cookies	Sesame seeds
Powdered fruit drinks	Crackers	Freeze-dried dinners	Pies	Soy beans
Cereals	Cookies	Prepackaged dinners	Cheesecake	Wheat germ
Granola	Chocolate bars	Rice	Pudding	Raisins and other dried fruits
Oatmeal	Dried fruits	Lentils		Popcorn
Hot cereals	Bagels	Beans		Soups
Powdered milk	Peanut butter	Potato flakes		Instant sauces
Dried fruits	Candy bars	Vegetable flakes		Bouillon cubes
Pancakes	Soups	Tuna		Spices
Muffins	Hot cocoa	Cheese		Maple syrup
Bannock bread	Coffee	Sausage, bacon, or ham		Honey
Sausage, bacon, or ham	Tea	Tortillas		Brown sugar
Butter or margarine		Soup mixes		Soy sauce
Brown sugar		Instant sauces		
Honey		Butter or margarine		
Maple syrup		Cooking oil		

Water

Cold winter air is extremely dry, and because of this your moisture loss is more acute in winter than in summer. Replenish the water you lose through perspiration and breathing by drinking constantly. While you may not feel thirsty, force yourself to drink before you become dehydrated. If you drink 3 or 4 quarts of water every day, you'll feel more energetic and healthier during your trip. Dehydration can lead to depression, lethargy, chills, and hypothermia. An easy way to tell if you're getting enough water is to check your urine. If it's dark, you need to drink more.

Chapter 9

On Trail

"This is it," you say quietly to yourself, stealing a quick glance around to see how the others are doing and to see if they feel the same nervous excitement that you feel. It's hard to tell—everyone is so intent on arranging their packs, buckling boots, and putting on or taking off layers.

You get out of the car and feel the cool, fresh breeze against your cheek and follow the snow-covered trail with your eyes into the forest to where it disappears. You linger for a moment, reluctant to give up the warmth and safety of the vehicle. With a flash you see that you're astride a margin, about to cross a boundary into the unknown. Suddenly, you understand that this trip is no longer theoretical. One more step and you're committed.

"Everybody ready? Okay, let's go!"

Pacing

After about ten seconds, apprehension turns to exhilaration. The simple act of moving engenders powerful feelings of freedom, joy, and wonder. You've crossed the barrier; all doubts are gone, replaced by sheer excitement.

For the first half hour or so, you burn up the track, carried by adrenaline and excitement. After a while, however, you adjust to the new surroundings. The car and the road are far behind. Life settles down to a more natural rhythm. You feel the first flush of heat, know that you're about to break a sweat, and stop. Time to take off a layer or two, slow down, and move along at a regular pace.

On the trail, find a comfortable pace that you can keep up all day without stopping. Going full tilt until your legs feel like lead, your lungs are on fire, and your heart is thumping like a battering ram is no way to enjoy yourself. When you stop, it should be only to take a drink of water, shed or add a layer, look at the map, or grab a handful of gorp. If you need to stop to rest, it's a sure sign that you're moving too quickly.

It's important to realize that for the first day or two you'll be adjusting to a whole new world and way of living. Give yourself a chance to get acclimated, not only to your surroundings, but also to your equipment. Don't try to cover too much ground the first day or so, but leave time for adjusting your clothing and packing systems, fiddling with bindings and skins, and setting up camp in the light.

Thermo-Regulation

We're talking about layering again. Remember, the trick is to stay dry. Most beginning winter campers can't fathom needing only a layer or two while on the trail, but it's true: Much of the time when you're moving along, you'll wear only your long underwear top and tights.

While in camp, before heading out in the morning, anticipate how much clothing you'll need after ten minutes of vigorous hiking or skiing and strip down before you set out. After a few minutes, the chill you feel will be replaced by a luxurious warm glow as your muscles warm to the task ahead. And if you need to stop to take off another layer, do it; don't be shy. Better to make a few adjustments early on than to get soaked.

An important reminder: Keep all your layers dry! Brush snow off everything. If it's snowing, put on your shell. If you stop for lunch in the sun or build a small fire, take advantage of the heat to dry your clothes. Never let a drying opportunity pass by without taking it.

Staying Together

There are times members of your group will want to spread out to give each other some space and to ski or snowshoe alone for awhile. On these occasions you can really tune in to your environment. Look around and listen, learn what the wilderness has to teach, but always stay within sight and sound of each other.

An easy way to stay in touch is if everyone takes responsibility for the person directly behind. This way, from front to back there's an unbroken line of communication. If anyone needs to stop to shed a layer or take a drink, the whole group should pause. No one gets left behind.

When traveling in potentially hazardous places, the group should

A winter camping group in the Alaskan wilderness on a warm morning in May

keep close together in case anyone needs help. There will be times—for instance, when you cross thin ice or a possible avalanche chute—when communication will be vital. At these and other times the group needs to work together as a team.

The group must travel at the pace of the slowest member. If the group exceeds this pace, the slow member will become fatigued and more susceptible to illness or injury. How do you keep the slowest person from becoming demoralized or from dropping too far behind? Let that person lead the group for a while. The psychological boost a person gets from being out in front, breaking trail in fresh snow, can have an enormously beneficial effect. Especially when approaching a summit or open vista, let the person who spends most of the time in the rear have a chance to get there first. The view from up front can be a lot more interesting than the scene from the rear.

Rotating the person in the lead can accomplish another purpose as well: breaking trail. If the snow is deep, this can be an exhausting chore. One way to spread out the work is to travel single file. When the person in front gets tired, he or she steps to the side, lets the rest of the group pass, and then takes a new position at the rear. By the time the rest of the group members have done their turn at the front of the line, the rear person should be well rested from skiing or snowshoeing on a broken trail so that he or she can once again take over the lead position.

Another way to break trail more easily is to lighten the load of one group member by dividing his heavy food and equipment among the rest of the group, then let this person go ahead and break the trail for his more heavily burdened teammates. The light pack can be traded around so everyone has a chance to contribute to the effort. When everyone takes turns breaking trail, all members feel they're adding to the overall goals of the group.

Awareness

The best way for the group to avoid trouble and have a pleasant trip is for everyone to be aware. Preventing injuries is vital on any trip, but it is especially important in winter. Through acute awareness of the group's surroundings and of each other, you can greatly enhance your chances for an incident-free experience.

When you're aware, you can read the signals nature is sending. For example, dark or discolored snow on the surface of a river or lake speaks of thin ice or overflowing water. A ring around the moon tells of an approaching storm. A steep, open snow gully through a forested slope delivers a lecture on avalanches. Snow streamers blowing off a summit carry the message of windchill and certain frostbite for uncovered skin.

There are many indications of potential trouble, many clues to the right path. Listen to and study your surroundings, and listen to notice each other too. A person often can't see the signs of frostbite on him- or herself: the whiteness on his or her cheeks or nose. Someone else must be aware. If someone complains of being tired, cold, or hungry, it's a clear indication that something is amiss and must be dealt with immediately, before complications develop.

Look around, keep your eyes and ears open, and be aware. Someone is trying to tell you something.

Navigation

Moving confidently through the wilderness toward a destination and knowing exactly where you are the entire time is called navigation. No one is born with the ability to navigate a course through unknown territory. Doing so requires skill and training.

With a map, compass, altimeter, and awareness of surroundings, a wilderness traveler is never lost, even though she may be seeing the country for the first time. Striking off in any direction and letting go of the security of roads, crowds, and even trails is a liberating feeling. All it takes to feel at home in the wild is the right tools and a sense of where you are.

In the United States, finding true wilderness to navigate is becoming more difficult every year. Outside of Alaska, there are perhaps a handful of places more than a dozen miles from a road, and that number is shrinking. Our national forests are crisscrossed by a labyrinth of logging roads; our national parks are home to a network of scenic drives and visitor's concessions. Even our official wilderness areas are liberally laced with maintained footpaths and sprinkled with trail signs. The ability to navigate in unmarked terrain can get you off trail and into those last reserves of truly wild country. Indeed, navigation may soon be the art of getting lost—getting away from it all!

The first step toward becoming a skilled navigator is to develop your powers of observation. Notice which way the streams run, where the lakes are, and if any hills or mountains rise above the surrounding landscape. Notice gaps, or passes, between the ranges. Keep an eye out for areas devoid of vegetation, such as bogs, meadows, or open summits. Turn around completely and observe how these landmarks appear when you approach them from another direction. Watch the sun rise in the east and set in the west. The moon does the same, as do the stars—and the North Star hangs over the North Pole, making it an exceptional navigational aid.

The landscape is a complex maze, but it has a pattern and a rhythm. Immerse yourself in it and observe. Try to understand how it's all laid out. Throughout your trip, continue to watch the landscape as it unfolds before you.

The Map

The best maps for use in the backcountry are the topographic maps put out by the United States Geological Survey (USGS) and the Canada Map Office. Topographic maps are especially useful because the contour lines indicate variations in elevation. By looking at the contour lines, you can tell whether the surface is flat, rolling, or steep.

Where the contour lines are far apart, the terrain is gently rolling or almost flat. You can tell this is so because the contour interval, or the space between the contour lines, is wide. If, for example, the contour interval (indicated at the bottom of the map) is 20 feet, that means there's a 20-foot difference in elevation between every contour line. Traveling over an area where the contour lines are drawn far apart on the map will be easy. The terrain will be gentle and the elevation change may be barely noticeable.

Where the contour lines are bunched together, the terrain is steep: The elevation gains indicated by the contour lines are right next to each other. When traveling over terrain described on the map by closely drawn contour lines, you'll not have to go far to experience rapid changes in elevation. An extremely steep pitch, such as a cliff, will be represented on a topographic map by contour lines that are right on top of one another.

It's also important to know how contour lines indicate the direction water flows. Without this knowledge, you may not know which way to follow a stream out of the mountains or how to use it as a reference point. The valley of streams, creeks, and rivers is always indicated by a V, with the apex, or meeting, of the two branches of the V pointing *upstream*, because streams are always located between ridges or heights of land. Where the contour lines of the ridges on either side of the stream come

Consult your topo maps whenever you stop on trail.

together they form the letter V unless the valley is broad, in which case the contour lines outlining it may take the shape of a U. Whether U or V, however, it's important to know that the apex always points upstream.

As described, the contour lines on either side of the stream show the ridges rising from either side of it. These are indicated by a U shape if the shoulder of the ridge is rounded, or by a V shape if the ridge is sharp. It's important to remember, whatever the shape, that the apex of the U or V always points *downhill*.

Map Symbols

Once you understand contour lines so that the hills and ridges pop up off the map as if they were three-dimensional, the next step is to interpret the colors and symbols on the map. Once you can do this, using a map will be virtually the same as viewing the terrain from above—as though you were looking down on it from an airplane.

Though the world in winter is monochromatic compared to summer, and though your aerial view as represented by your view of the map will be a summer one, you can easily make the mental adjustment. Green areas on the map indicate places that are forested or covered with vegetation. Blue, not surprisingly, shows water. White areas are places that are perennially devoid of vegetation. These could be permanent snowfields, glaciers, open rock outcrops, or even paved areas such as parking lots or airfields. Black indicates man-made features such as buildings, radio towers, and mines. Secondary roads are also black, while highways are red. Single dashed black lines denote trails. Double dashed black lines indicate jeep trails or logging roads.

An important point to remember—especially where old trails, logging roads, and cabins are concerned—is that some features aren't permanent. Logging roads, for example, are notoriously poor reference points because once the timber is cut and hauled away, the roads are sometimes abandoned and they become overgrown. If the map has not been field checked in a decade or two, the roads may have vanished.

Using the Map in the Field

Paying close attention to your surroundings will make you a skilled map reader. Matching the natural features to the features as they appear on the map will soon be as simple as reading a road map. The process of converting three-dimensional, natural features into their two-dimensional representations is the same in the woods as it is on the highway. Now instead of looking for the freeway exit, you'll be keeping an eye out for the stream crossing.

By carefully following your progress on the map, matching the terrain around you to the terrain on the map, you'll know exactly where you are. You should have no more use for your compass than you have when driving your car. Ninety percent of your traveling will be done this way. But be certain to bring along the compass for the remaining 10 percent.

The Compass

Every winter camper should carry a compass and know how to use it. The best compass for wilderness navigation is a handy, inexpensive little item that consists of a free-floating magnetic needle in a clear liquid rotating housing, an orienting arrow and parallel north-south lines engraved within the rotating housing, a clear plastic base plate, a rotating dial calibrated in 1- or 2-degree increments, a direction-of-travel arrow engraved on the plastic base plate, and an index line at the foot of the direction-of-travel arrow, where you read the number of degrees from the rotating dial.

Initially, map and compass work can be complicated. It's useful to obtain a basic compass and a topographic map to practice with before setting out into the wilderness.

The most basic use for a compass is to travel in a straight line toward a destination. For example, if you see a peak off in the distance, point your compass's direction-of-travel arrow at the summit, then rotate the compass housing until the red end of the magnetic needle is floating directly over the orienting arrow. Now look at the point where the rotating dial lines up with the direction-of-travel arrow and the index line, and notice the degree. This is your magnetic bearing. You can follow the magnetic bearing directly to the peak by walking straight ahead.

If you travel through areas where you can no longer actually see your destination, a good way to stay on course is to point the direction-of-travel arrow at trees, rocks, or other objects that are on your magnetic bearing in line with your destination. Also, have your teammates go ahead of you on your magnetic bearing and then sight on them. Move up to where they are and send them out again. In this fashion you can move quickly and easily toward your goal without straying from your magnetic bearing.

Which North?

The needle of your compass aligns itself with the earth's magnetic field, pointing in the direction of the magnetic North Pole. Though it wanders, the magnetic North Pole is presently located west-northwest of Sverdrup Island in the Canadian Arctic, hundreds of miles to the south of the geographic North Pole. The difference between these two North Poles is called declination.

Unless you're traveling along the agonic line—the line of 0 degrees declination passing through the center of the continent (running from the true North Pole, skirting the east side of Hudson Bay, cutting through central Ontario, and passing down through Indiana and western Florida), where the variation between magnetic north and true north is 0 degrees—you'll have to account for declination whenever you use your map and compass together. In some places, the variation is significant, and a failure to account for declination will lead you far astray from your intended course.

In eastern and western parts of the U.S., for example, declination reaches 20 degrees. In northern Canada, it can be 40 degrees or more. A compass error of only 1 degree translates into an error of about 90 feet per mile on the ground. If you were to head for a landmark 2 miles distant in an area where the declination was 30 degrees and failed to account for the variation, you would miss your objective by over a mile!

Because the agonic line runs roughly through the center of the continent, it's easy to remember that if you're east of the line, your compass needle will point to the west of true north (declination west). If you are west of the line, your compass will point to the east of true north (declination east). The farther you are from the line, the greater the declination will be.

In the margin of all USGS and Canada Map Office topographic maps there's a diagram showing the declination. A line pointing to the North Star indicates true north. The borders of the map also indicate true north. The east and west borders of the map are lines of longitude. They lie along a true north-south line. Magnetic north is shown as a line with an arrow. The numerical value of the declination is indicated on the diagram.

Using Map and Compass Together

From map to field. If you want to follow a compass bearing toward a destination that you can't see, you'll not be able to follow a magnetic bearing, as you did in the earlier example. You'll have to take a bearing from your map.

Let's say you're in northern Maine, where the declination is about 20 degrees west, and you want to plot a course from where you are (point A) to where you want to go (point B). Here's an easy way to do this.

1. Place your map flat on the ground (no need to orient it), then locate your position (point A) and your destination (point B).

2. Using the edge of the compass base plate as a ruler, draw a straight line between the two points.

3. Next, forgetting about the magnetic needle because we're seeking a true north bearing instead of a magnetic bearing, align the base plate of your compass on the line that intersects points A and B, with the direction-of-travel arrow pointing toward B.

4. Turn the compass housing so the n and the engraved orienting arrow point to true north (the top of the map) and the engraved north-south lines are parallel to the east and west borders of the map.

5. Now read the bearing at the index line at the foot of the direction-of-travel arrow. This is your true-north bearing. All that remains is to translate this true bearing into a magnetic bearing so you can use your compass to follow it.

Because in this example your compass's magnetic needle points 20 degrees to the west of this true bearing, you'll need to compensate. You can do this by adding the value of the declination to your true bearing: Rotate the calibrated dial counterclockwise until you've added 20 degrees. If you're west of the agonic line, your magnetic needle will point too far east, so you must subtract the declination to get a true bearing.

In the eastern part of the continent, when converting a bearing from map to compass, I remember to *add* because there are more letters in the word *compass* than in the word *map*. Other people use rhymes to remember how to convert a bearing from map to compass, such as "Declination east is least (subtract), declination west is best (add)."

Now you've translated your reading from the map to an actual direction in the field. Pick up the compass, hold it steady at your waist, and turn your body until the magnetic needle aligns itself over the engraved orienting arrow. Your direction-of-travel arrow is now pointing directly toward point B, indicating precisely the way you should go, though you have yet to actually see your destination.

From field to map. You're hiking along a trail in northern Maine, and suddenly you come to a clearing. Off in the distance you see a sharp peak rising above all the others in the range. Just for fun, you take the opportunity to locate your precise location on the trail. Here's what you do.

1. Hold your compass steady at your waist and point the direction-of-travel arrow right at the summit of the peak.

2. Rotate the compass housing until the orienting arrow is directly beneath the magnetic needle, then read the magnetic bearing at the index line at the foot of the direction-of-travel arrow. In this instance it reads 90 degrees. But you know that the declination is 20 degrees west and that when you try to transfer this bearing to the map, it will be 20 degrees off. You need to subtract 20 degrees when converting this magnetic bearing into a true bearing on the map.

3. So rotate the calibrated dial clockwise and subtract 20 degrees. Now the number opposite the direction-of-travel arrow reads 70 degrees.

4. To locate yourself on the map, place the base plate on the summit of the peak and turn the compass until the magnetic needle is aligned over the orienting arrow. Using the base plate as a ruler, draw a line from the peak to where it intersects the trail. You're located precisely where that line and the trail intersect.

Again, in the western part of the U.S. and Canada, the situation is the reverse. Because the declination is east, when you want to transfer the magnetic bearing to the map, you'll have to add the declination.

Facility with map and compass requires lots of practice. Most backcountry travelers need to brush up on their skills every time they set out on a trip. The saying "Use it or lose it" certainly applies to wilderness navigation.

Altimeter

Most of us haven't given much thought to carrying an altimeter on our winter wilderness forays. Instead, we happily choose to forego yet another expensive piece of high-tech gear.

Yet there are things an altimeter can tell us that a mere compass and map cannot. Suppose you're hurrying off a mountain in poor visibility, heading down a ridge in a featureless area where landmarks are few. You know that a gully off to the left will deliver you to safety, but which one?

They all look alike in the gloom, and the wrong choice could be disastrous.

By checking your map and reading the contour line, you can tell that the gully you need is at an elevation of, say, 8,500 feet. Arriving at what you believe is your gully, you check the terrain, your map, and your altimeter. The instrument confirms what the terrain and the map suggest: You've found your route.

In addition to being a navigational aid, the altimeter can help you read the weather. Because an altimeter measures air pressure to calculate altitude, it is, in effect, a barometer. This means an altimeter can also alert you to the changing weather patterns associated with incoming high- and low-pressure systems. A rising air pressure usually means fair weather; falling air pressure means unsettled or stormy weather ahead. This information may be helpful to you in planning your day's travel.

As with all technology, remember that you can't just blindly trust your altimeter. It's sort of like Heisenberg's uncertainty principle (you remember that one, don't you?): You

With an altimeter you can pinpoint your location by checking the reading against the elevation contour lines on a topo map. *Photograph courtesy of Brunton.*

can't track both altitude and barometric pressure with a single tool. If you do, you might find yourself going to sleep at 10,500 feet but waking up at 11,500 feet, according to your altimeter. In all likelihood, a storm rolled in as you slept, and with it the barometric pressure fell. This is why it's important to check and reset your altimeter whenever you're at a confirmed elevation, such as the top of a mountain or where the trail crosses a stream.

Bushwhacking

Snow has a way of obliterating heavily used footpaths, small rock cairns, and blazes, returning a sense of the primeval to even the most popular summer routes. Every step in fresh snow might as well be the first.

You don't need to go off trail to escape the crowds and find solitude in winter, but trails don't necessarily go everywhere you want to travel. Just because someone laid out a trail a long time ago doesn't mean you must stick to it. Some of the best views, deepest gorges, highest waterfalls, and tallest stands of ancient forest are off trail.

Bushwhacking can take you there. To go off trail you'll need sharp navigational skills and an intense awareness of your surroundings. Bring maps and compasses—and use them—but also be aware of the sun and its position in the sky. Look around often to get a fix on where you are. Frequently check your progress against distant peaks or ridges. Match these to the terrain featured on your map.

When bushwhacking, take several precautions for safety: For eye protection, it's not a bad idea to wear glasses or goggles in thick brush, and keep your thumbs outside of the wrist straps on your ski poles. In addition, be aware of where you place your poles; pole baskets can get caught on roots or branches as you ski or snowshoe by, pulling you off balance and causing you to take a tumble. Finally, look out for spruce traps—areas where fallen timber has been covered with snow, hiding the deep holes between the interlacing trunks.

When searching out the best off-trail route, don't stick to a beeline course. Move around—swing left, then right—and look for the least obstructed, most hassle-free route. Too often, novice bushwhackers stick to their compass course and never deviate. As long as you know where you are and where you need to go, give yourself some latitude to maneuver through rough country.

Wildlife Encounters

One January day while on expedition on northern Maine's frozen West Branch of the Penobscot River, I was out ahead of the group, breaking trail, unencumbered by a heavy sled for a turn. I felt so light that the foot of fresh snow couldn't slow me down. Skiing along at a good clip, I first heard the ravens croak, then saw them flapping heavily away from me, heading downriver and out of sight.

Rounding a bend, I saw two large eastern coyotes raise their heads, look at me, then bolt across the ice and snow into the spruce and disappear. But there was something left lying on the ice where they had been only a moment before. I skied the last hundred yards or so, and the story of what had happened unfolded as I read the tracks in the snow.

In northern latitudes, wildlife remains active in winter, as shown by these fresh polar bear tracks in northern Labrador.

Snow School

What was the coldest temperature ever recorded in the United States?

The coldest temperature ever recorded in the United States was −79.8 degrees at Prospect Creek, Alaska, on January 23, 1971. •

The deer they'd run down was still warm when I reached the place, though the coyotes were making quick work of the remains. It was easy to see where they'd cut the deer out of the forest and forced it onto the ice so that, through agility, skill, and teamwork, they could finally bring it down.

Looking off to where the coyotes had vanished, I could feel their eyes on me, waiting patiently but hungrily for me to move on. I wished them well, then left them to their meal, feeling elated at having witnessed this ancient yet timeless ritual.

Although northern forests are widely considered to be lands that support large wildlife populations, this image is incorrect. It's only because humans have depleted the more bountiful wildlife resources that formerly existed across most of the continent that this popular misconception persists. In fact, the northern forests are among the poorest of natural environments where wildlife is concerned. Here, animal populations are dispersed because the food sources they exploit are so marginal and so widely distributed. Northern animals need vast, uninterrupted areas as habitat, requiring much more range than animals in more benign environments. Further, these animals are only occasionally abundant, because they're subject to population fluctuations and they're extremely sensitive to environmental change, habitat loss, and overexploitation. Incompatible human activity such as timber cutting, road building, and housing development can send a population crashing.

That said, winter is perhaps the best time to see wildlife. Animals are more easily spotted in the monochromatic landscape, they tend to stick to well-traveled corridors, and their tracks indicate who they are, how many they are, where they're going, and when they passed by. If you watch for signs and learn animals' habits, there's a good chance you'll see wildlife on your trips.

Through these encounters, you can gain a new respect and understanding for animals. When you spend time out in the snow and cold and meet another warm-blooded creature trying to make a living in the winter environment, you realize how closely related you are, how much you share and have in common. Remember that winter is a critical period for animals because food sources are extremely scarce, and as a consequence their energy reserves are very low.

Disturbing animals in winter—causing them to run or otherwise expend valuable energy reserves—is harmful and ultimately may even kill them. If you encounter animals, keep your distance; it's a good idea to give them plenty of space, and don't alarm them.

Build in Time for Enjoyment

If you just put your head down and doggedly push forward on the trail day after day, you may accomplish your mission, but chances are you won't have a lot of fun. Build in time to relax. A day off now and then is a perfect way to rest, take day trips unencumbered by heavy packs, and enjoy your surroundings.

Chapter 10

Backcountry Skiing and Riding

We should get one thing straight at the outset: You don't need to be an expert skier or rider to enjoy backcountry ski touring and camping, but it helps to be comfortable on skis or a snowboard. You can choose tours that are less difficult and still enjoy a wilderness tour, but enjoying the whole range of backcountry skiing and riding opportunities takes lots of practice.

Yet as Steve Barnett, noted backcountry skier and author suggests, there are skills that are even more important to master: "Good ski technique rates well behind avalanche knowledge, navigational skills, and camping skills as something you need to know" in order to enjoy a fun, safe winter ski or split-board touring experience.

Many winter campers choose skis and split boards because they're versatile, efficient means of transportation. And while it's true that skis and boards can also be a heck of a lot of fun, it isn't required that you be a backcountry powder hound, sniffing out every delectable back bowl, to become an accomplished winter camper. If you should ever want to drop the pack in camp and cut loose, however, whooping it up in the white stuff, it's nice to know you can.

At this point in time, all backcountry skiers and riders in North America use free-heel bindings for the majority of their time on the snow, which is on the tour itself. Whether you're on alpine touring skis, telemark skis, or a split board, these bindings mean your heels aren't locked down during the tour.

Backcountry skiing and riding is different from the fare on piste at a lift-served resort. With the flexibility provided by a free heel, you can go up, down, or across a trail with equal ease. Also, because you're in the backcountry, there are no restrictions on where to go. If you want to bank turns through the birches or leave your autograph on a pristine blanket of backcountry powder, go for it! There's no "out of bounds." Of course, there's no tilling and grooming either. What you see is what you get, and the backcountry skier and rider is faced with a kaleidoscope of conditions, from perfect fluff to breakable crust.

That said, many lift-served ski areas in both northern New England and the West have ample off-trail backcountry skiing and riding within their permit boundaries. This inbounds backcountry is the perfect place to hone your backcountry skiing and riding skills.

Skiing and Riding Are Basically the Same

Whether you're a telemarker, someone who alpine tours, or a rider, the basics of getting up and down the mountain are essentially the same. Sure, the first always has a free heel; the second has a locked heel on the downhills, and the descent for the third is on one board instead of two. As we'll see, though, as far as the essentials go, it doesn't matter what you use for sliding.

The Fundamentals

Attitude. To become the best backcountry skier and rider you can possibly be, you need to develop a very positive and confident attitude. The best skiers and riders constantly push themselves to the edge of their abilities. On every turn they monitor all their motions, making instantaneous technical adjustments whenever necessary in order to maintain perfect balance while crisply moving from turn to turn in any snow and on any terrain.

Stance. As in all athletic endeavors, you'll need to strike the proper pose in skiing or riding. In order to make swift movements and react to changing terrain features, you'll need to assume the proper stance. Visualize a soccer goalie prepared to block the shot. That's basically the position you want to be in.

Your weight should be placed solidly on both feet, and your ankles and knees should be flexed. Your feet should be hip-width apart so that your body is properly aligned from your shoulders through your hips and right on down to your ankles. Keep your head up, with your eyes scanning the terrain ahead, and lean forward slightly with your hands up and in front of you, where you can see them.

That's a stable, athletic skiing and riding stance. Now you're ready to slide.

Hands. As we've discovered, your hands should be up and in front where you can see them. They're crucial to your balance, and hands in this "ready" position help to keep you in the proper forward, solid stance. If your hands are down by your sides, it's essentially impossible to maintain a proper stance. Low hands, and especially hands that end up behind you, will throw you off balance and cause you either to fall or to fail to execute the next turn. If you keep your hands within your peripheral vision, you'll stay forward, balanced, and reactive to the terrain.

Balance. Many skiers and riders lose their balance by becoming hesitant at the end of a turn, especially on challenging terrain. Instead of aggressively moving forward toward the next turn, they shy away from it, letting their hands and hips fall back, which immediately yanks them out of their centered stance and into what's called the backseat.

To avoid the backseat, move forward assertively toward your next turn. Stay relaxed, but at the same time scrupulously maintain the proper stance and hand position. Press your shins into the tongues of your boots to maintain an aggressive forward-leaning position.

Keep your head up and look forward toward your next turn, not down at the snow right in front of you. Constantly scan and evaluate both the terrain and the snow you're about to encounter. Monitor your stance and balance, make quick adjustments to stay balanced and centered over your feet at the end of each turn, and then immediately look toward the next one.

Feet. It's important to feel the snow with your feet. As we've discussed, the best skiers and riders monitor their every motion. Their brains are like on-board diagnostic computers scrutinizing all of their mechanics, searching for flaws. At the same time, they're constantly evaluating information transmitted from the snow through their skis or board to their feet—and they adjust their technique according to these subtle messages. Your feet can tell you all you need to know about the sliding surface and whether or not you need to make split-second changes in your technique. Look ahead to see what you're getting into, but strive to develop a feel for the nuances of snow.

Visualization. Skiing and riding are not only very physically active sports, but they're also highly mentally active sports.

Visualization is one of the easiest ways to improve your skills and improve your performance on the snow. For example, all ski and snowboard racers visualize the course and the line they plan to take through the gates before they enter the starting gate. By imagining themselves with perfect form on the course, and by replaying those mental images again and again, the racers know exactly what to do and how to do it when the actual moment arises.

When you find yourself in a technically difficult situation—a very steep section of a slope, for example—visualize exactly how you plan to ski or ride it. Once you know precisely what moves you want to make and are confident you can make them exactly as you've visualized, you're ready to jump in.

Flow. Skiing and riding are paradoxical. They require you to be both very disciplined and very relaxed in your stance. They demand that you

Note this skier's strong, aggressive stance, with the hands placed forward and up, where he can see them.

confront the terrain with confidence and that you're also receptive to the slightest fine changes. They ask that you make your performance look effortless, but in reality, both require you to be a perpetual motion machine. To be an excellent skier and rider, you must be constantly in motion as you flow down the slope, just like a river flowing between its banks. To do this, you must stay dynamic. Flow from turn to turn with continuous motion and absolutely no hesitation when you change direction. Even a microsecond's hesitation between ending your last turn and beginning a new one will throw you ever so slightly off balance and stop the flow. You flow in your skiing and riding by making your next turn a seamless extension of your last turn.

Make a few turns and then check your tracks in the snow. If you see any sections between turns that look flat and straight, as opposed to sinuous, then you're hesitating between turns. In fact, you're traversing between turns, if only for a split second. Eliminate the hesitation, develop a smooth rhythm, and you'll ski and ride with flow.

As with skiing, a solid, athletic stance is crucial to backcountry snowboarding.

Skiing and Riding with a Pack

Skiing and riding with a pack requires that you de-emphasize many of your skiing motions. The added mass and movement of the pack can contribute to some mighty crashes until you learn to use finesse. Be careful to maintain a flexed, athletic stance, and keep your hands up where you can see them.

On downhills remember that the results of even slight adjustments to

Skiing with a heavy pack requires finesse and balance.

your posture will be greatly magnified while you're wearing a pack; so strive for flow while making smooth adjustments to changes in the terrain.

Skiing and Split Boarding with a Sled

Skiing and riding with a loaded sled are easier than skiing and riding with a heavy backpack. With a sled, you don't carry the weight high on your back, so it isn't as critical to de-emphasize your motions. The sled is pulled from your hips, which happen to be at or very near your balance point, so you don't have to worry about restraining your motion to avoid throwing yourself off balance.

On moderate downhills, if the sled has a rigid harness system, it'll track behind you so that your downhill motions are basically unchanged. As ski patrollers demonstrate daily, skiing and riding with a loaded sled is possible even on steep sections.

On supersteep downhills, where rapid, successive changes of direction are required, the sled is out of its element. The sled will not be able to match your rapid turns, and its weight will force you down the slope faster than you probably intend to go. In this case, attach a brake rope to the rear of the sled and have someone hold on to the rope to keep it from barreling out of control. If you're by yourself, lower the sled from above down the steep parts, using the rope.

Handling Tough Conditions

In the backcountry you're going to run across the whole range of snow and ice conditions—sometimes in the same day. You may also confront difficult sections of slopes that will test your skills and your confidence in your ability to make the descent.

Every backcountry skier and rider has had to confront fear and doubt at one point or another. In these cases, what do you do?

If the situation is clearly way beyond your skill level or is otherwise obviously foolhardy and dangerous, then by all means retreat and find another way down. If it's not beyond your true ability, however, and you want to give it a try, now is the time to put all of your hard-won skills to the test.

The most important factor in tough conditions is the right attitude. Be confident, and visualize yourself succeeding. In your mind review your stance, your hand position, and your balance. See yourself making controlled, round turns with no hesitation. When you've rehearsed each move in your mind several times and know you can do it, relax, breathe deeply, and give it a try.

Snowshoeing Technique

It's fun to see people approach snowshoeing for the first time. There must be some trick to this, they think. What is it? Where do I sign up for lessons?

I like the way writer Nathaniel Reade describes snowshoeing technique: "Snowshoeing is idiotically simple: You strap on the suckers and you walk. End of story."

Reade is right. On the flats, just walk normally; there's no need to waddle along like a duck. Newcomers to the sport look as though they're doing a John Wayne swagger or imitating a drunken sailor on a pitching ship's deck. There's really no need for theatrics.

When climbing steep pitches, kick step with your snowshoes. The crampons underfoot will bite the snow and give you good grip. If you're crossing a slope, use the edges of the snowshoes like the edges of skis and angle your body into the slope, just as you would if you were skiing or riding.

As Nathaniel Reade says: "Snowshoeing is idiotically simple. You strap on the suckers and you walk. End of story."

Most people use ski poles when snowshoeing. (See chapter 7.) Poles offer tremendous advantages when you're striding, climbing, or descending.

Using Crampons

For climbing steep, icy pitches or traversing open summits, crampons (see chapter 7) may be necessary. Those who plan on doing winter traveling in the mountains should bring them along or else plan on avoiding these areas. Even skiers and snowshoers will discover that crampons can make it much easier to travel in the occasional stretch of tough, icy conditions.

Most crampons used by winter mountaineers have 12 points—10 under the ball and heel of the foot and 2 protruding at the front. The addition

Put on your crampons for climbing steep, icy slopes.

of the two front points allows for a technique called front pointing, or kicking the crampons directly into the snow or ice to form a step or platform to stand on.

When using crampons, keep your feet as flat as possible to gain maximum benefit from the points. Some climbers have a tendency to use the inside points when climbing or traversing a steep stretch. Unlike skiing, in which edging and angulation work to your benefit, this practice often results a fall caused when the points shear away the ice or snow underfoot.

Crampons are either rigid or hinged under the foot. For the winter camper, hinged crampons are the best choice because they can be used with a variety of footwear, from rigid plastic climbing boots to telemark ski boots with toe flex. Hinged crampons can be used even with soft snowboard boots and probably even with mukluks, whereas rigid crampons may be used only with stiff-soled boots. (They'll break if they're used with flexible footwear.)

When you walk with crampons, be careful not to spear your pant leg or gaiter with your front points. Everyone does it, but be careful. In addition, avoid stepping on climbing ropes if they're in use. And be sure to account for the additional 1½ inches or so of clearance you'll need when stepping over rocks; otherwise you'll catch the spikes and trip yourself.

Using an Ice Ax

For all but the most technical routes, ski poles are perfectly adequate when hiking or climbing with crampons. Even so, if your route plan calls for climbing or traversing steep, icy stretches, an ice ax will come in handy. Most backpacks now come equipped with ice-ax loops so that you can carry the ax securely and retrieve it when necessary. Because an ice ax can be extremely dangerous if used improperly, be sure to seek out proper training from qualified instructors before using it in the field.

The safest way to carry an ice ax is to grip the ax at the balance point halfway down the shaft, with the spike pointing forward and the pick pointing down. If the ax is to be used as a cane, grip it by placing your hand over the head, with your thumb around the adze and your fingers curled around the pick, which should be pointing to the rear.

If you're crossing a dangerous area where you may have to self-arrest— that is, stop your slide down a slope—grip the ax by placing one hand firmly upon the shaft above the spike. The other hand grips the head, with the thumb under the adze and the fingers securely wrapped around the pick. Position the ice-ax shaft diagonally across the chest from shoulder to opposite hip. Stop your slide by driving the pick into the snow using your upper-body weight. Press on the shaft with your shoulders and chest. Pulling up on the end of the shaft while pressing on it with your upper body will put additional pressure on the pick to drive it more securely into the snow.

If you're *not* wearing crampons and you go for a steep slide, keep your legs straight and dig into the snow with your feet to create additional drag. If you *are* wearing crampons, keep them away from the surface of the snow until you've almost stopped your slide, otherwise they may catch in the snow. Instead, use your knees to dig in and create additional friction.

Whatever position you're in when you begin your slide, always roll toward the pick to minimize the possibility of self-impalement. Never roll toward the spike because it may catch on the snow, dig in, and either be wrested from your hands or spin toward you at a dangerous angle.

Remember, if you fall, you'll generate a great deal of speed and force. Using sharp objects in these uncontrolled moments is very dangerous. It takes practice to be able to react properly and instantaneously before you gather too much speed.

Chapter 11

Rock and Ice

Mountains are alluring. The high country is challenging, remote, and mysterious. Mountains are also—relatively speaking—well protected by the laws of the United States and Canada. You have only to look at a map and notice where the crown jewels of our national park system are located to discover that mountains are a disproportionably well-represented ecological zone. They're harder to get to, their climate is usually harsh, and besides minerals, historically there has been less of commercial value in the highest, most forbidding ranges.

The lowlands are not as well protected, but they're even more important ecologically. Wetlands—rivers, lakes, and riparian woodlands—are the wellsprings of biological diversity, home to countless more species than the most spectacular alpine landscapes, and they offer some of the best winter tripping possibilities in North America.

Ice Travel

Traveling on an ice-covered river or chain of lakes is a great way to move through the winter wilderness. All across the north, whether for work or pleasure, travel over the frozen waterways was once a common practice. Currently, with roads and trails penetrating all but the wildest country and connecting points with the quickest, most direct route, ice travel is no longer as necessary, but there may not be a better way to cover long distances in winter; on a good day, you can cover 20 or even 30 miles on skis.

Traveling on ice is a pleasure. The wind-packed snow creates a smooth, fast surface, providing easy passage. Also, animals are aware of the advantage and tend to congregate in the river corridors, where they're easy to spot.

The river entices the traveler around each bend. Every wooded point, each rocky headland conceals some new mystery. Upon approach, the scene is revealed like the stage behind a rising curtain. To the Naskapi of Labrador the river is "the immemorial winter road," a way leading to the heart of the wild.

But as with other enticements, ice travel presents some hazards, and no experienced winter traveler ventures onto the ice without respect and perhaps a little fear. Even partial immersion in frigid water can cause at least delay to build a fire, warm up, and dry wet clothing. At worst, the danger can be much more serious. For these reasons it's imperative to approach all ice travel with caution and understand certain characteristics of ice.

Ice Characteristics

Ice that forms during a quick cold snap in late fall or early winter is called black ice, and when thick enough, it's a very safe travel surface. The ice is black because it freezes quickly without trapping air, slush, or gas. Black ice is strong and supple and will actually sag before breaking. When stressed, it sends a spider web of cracks running outward from the point of pressure, yet even then may remain intact. Because of this flexibility, it's often possible to retreat to firmer ice before breaking through black ice.

As winter progresses, black ice often incorporates snow into the top few inches and may turn cloudy gray or opaque. If cold temperatures prevail, this hard ice may reach a thickness of several feet. Strike it a blow, and it will respond with a solid-sounding thump. Hard ice is an excellent travel surface.

Beware of ice after a thaw or spring ice generally. Often saturated, this ice has a weakened structure due to repeated temperature changes. Spring ice may be in the process of rotting, becoming saturated and brittle, with a honeycomblike structure totally lacking in tensile strength. Consequently, it lacks the firmness and strength it possessed earlier in the season and can be quite dangerous. The bottom can fall out without warning, regardless of thickness.

General Ice Guidelines

Generally, 1 inch of black or hard ice will hold an average-sized person, but 2 inches are safer for this. Six inches will hold a moose, 8 inches a moose convention. Use your ski poles to tap ahead. The vibrations they send up your arms will tell you about ice thickness, structure, and strength. When traveling on suspect ice, carry a hatchet or an ice chisel and chip through the ice periodically to check thickness. Always check suspicious-looking ice before moving out onto it.

Become aware of the innumerable forms of ice and the factors that affect it. Experiment where you know the water is shallow and where you know you won't get wet if you break through. Study ice before you venture forth on your winter journey.

Ice Hazards

Learn the signs indicating danger.

- If animals deliberately avoid a stretch of ice, you should too. Animals know where the ice is thin and will go around it. Discolored snow on the surface may indicate the presence of water. If the snow looks dark or slushy, give that area a wide berth. A depression or slump in the snow cover in an otherwise uniform surface may indicate soft ice.

- Keep an eye out for tributary streams, and check your map for them. Their current will keep the ice open in even the coldest temperatures, sometimes for quite a distance. Plan to go to shore wherever a stream, even a small one, enters a river or exits a pond or lake.

- Ice that forms around a boulder or a tree stump may be unsafe. The eddy currents swirling behind these obstructions keep the ice from forming thick layers, resulting in a thin skin with air pockets beneath. Be extra careful of rapids and the outside bends of rivers where the current is moving quickly. The motion of the water may inhibit solid ice formation. Even underwater springs can swirl the water enough to keep it dangerous.

- Overflow, which is caused by water seeping up through cracks in the ice or over the edges near the banks, can saturate the snow cover and create a deep, wet slush or form a new layer of ice on top of the old one. If these newly formed ice sheaths are covered with snow but are not yet solid, you can plunge through them into the wet snow or water beneath—a good reason to tap ahead with a pole.

Your group should spread out when crossing suspect ice. Don't concentrate too much weight in one area. Unbuckle your pack or sled harness so you can shed them quickly if you fall in. Skis and snowshoes are excellent for keeping your weight distributed. You can also carry a long pole or branch to span a break should you fall in. (A 10- or 12-foot pole can be cut for this purpose.) If you're ever in a truly dangerous area where the ice is actually cracking, lie down and crawl away.

Remember that ice acts like a living surface. Even ice 2 and 3 feet thick will shift with its own weight, water levels, currents, wind, and temperature changes. At first these creaks, groans, and booming sounds will be unnerving, but you'll quickly learn to distinguish between ice that's merely shifting and ice that's truly dangerous.

The other common hazard of ice travel is wind. The surfaces of lakes and rivers are open and exposed and often windswept. The best precaution against windchill is to cover up. Use shell garments, a face mask, and goggles to keep the wind from frosting exposed skin.

A word here about ice navigation: On the snowy surfaces of rivers and lakes, navigation is essentially a simple matter of following the route as it unfolds before you. Portage trails, side streams, and islands can sometimes be confusing, but for the most part the shoreline is as good a guide to direction as the shoulder of a highway.

Ice Rescue

If someone does break through the ice, the whole group needs to act quickly as a team. Everyone will be prepared to deal with the situation if procedures have been discussed beforehand.

1. The first step, of course, is to make sure no one else is in imminent danger of crashing through the ice. Look around at each other; make sure everyone is on firm ice. If you're unsure, people should spread out their weight and crawl to safety.

2. Next, get a rope to the victim. On ice trips, some experienced travelers keep handy a river rescue throw rope for this purpose. Toss it to the victim just as you would to a capsized paddler in a rapid. The Styrofoam block and stuff sack that the rope is kept in and attached to will provide the victim with plenty to grip.

3. Then, span the edge of the breakthrough hole with skis or saplings. As the victim tries to climb out, he or she is likely to keep breaking the edge of the hole. The skis or saplings will distribute the pressure and give the victim something firm to climb on to. Slide the skis or saplings over the ice or crawl as far as possible to reach them toward the victim.

4. As soon as possible, quickly roll the victim in the snow to blot some

of the moisture he or she is carrying, and then get the victim out of the wind. Once sheltered from the wind, you can get the person out of wet clothes and into dry ones. If you have a large enough group, two people can be putting up a tent and building a fire before you arrive at the spot. Place the victim in a sleeping bag either inside the tent or outside to warm up by the fire. Keep the hot drinks coming, and make sure someone is with the victim at all times.

5. Finally, make sure everyone else is okay. You never know how people are going to react to an emergency. They can become quite frightened once a hazardous situation is under control.

Mountain Travel

Technical ice and snow climbing is beyond the scope of this book, but winter mountaineering—mountain travel on snowshoes and skis—is not. The range of the winter camper frequently extends to the realm of the high peaks. It's here, at and above tree line, that you'll find many of the most spectacular and intensely satisfying winter camping routes.

The mountains can require a level of concentration and skills much greater than those used to travel the forest or waterways. Navigation is no longer a simple matter of following the shoreline. Wind is constant and blows with greater velocity, and blizzards that obliterate all natural features and guides to direction are not uncommon. Also, avalanches are possible wherever there's a slope covered with snow.

Don't turn back now, however. Concentrate on developing sound judgment through experience, weigh your decisions heavily toward safety, and at first choose simple rather than complex routes. Gradually increase the level of difficulty as you acquire skills and expand your comfort zone.

Mountain Trails

It happens all the time. You're swinging along the trail, gradually gaining altitude, taking turns breaking the path, when you come upon a clearing or a stand of mature hardwood forest. Suddenly everyone stops moving.

"What's up?" someone asks from the back of the line.

"Trail's disappeared. It's gone."

"Can't just vanish. It's got to be here somewhere!"

Mountain trails in winter have a way of playing hide-and-seek. Once

For those who make the effort, the winter backcountry offers spectacular views.

Winter travelers ascend a remote peak in the Alaskan wilderness

you get the hang of the game, it can be a lot of fun. Until then, though, it's a source of stress and frustration.

I've led Outward Bound groups that panicked when the path hid itself on them. Without the thin line of security represented by the trail, they felt like castaways marooned in a hostile white wilderness. Perhaps even more, they resented their instructor's cheerful attitude. How could he not share their anxiety?

"Do you know where you are on the map?"

"Yes."

"Do you know which direction you're headed in?"

"Yes."

"Can you see how the trail follows this ridge on the map?"

"Yes."

"So what are you worried about?"

You don't need the trail to get from point A to point B. If you know where you are and know where you're going, you can usually strike out on your own and get there cross country. The advantage a trail offers is that it generally follows the easiest, most expedient route available between two points. This should be a clue to finding the lost path. Where would you go if you were a trail? Over the cliff or up the avalanche chute? Not likely.

As soon as you lose the path, stop. Retrace your steps to the last known point on your route. There are plenty of clues to find the missing trail; you just have to know what to look for.

The first thing you need to do is think about where you are. Are you on a ridge? Climbing midslope? In a valley? Confirm the terrain, and then check your map. Match natural features that surround you to those represented on the map—the brook you just crossed, for instance, or the fact that you're just below a col. Sure enough, when you look at the map, you'll see where the trail crosses a brook before climbing up to a narrow col. Of course, you must be right between the two points.

If there are no prominent features in your vicinity, you can always backtrack to one—an open ridge, a pass, a significant drainage—and locate yourself that way. Go back to your last known point on the trail and start sniffing around. Spread out and look for clues. Look critically at the trees for any unnatural openings or patterns. Often, the trail is revealed by a gap through the trunks. Also, look up at the canopy. Notice any gaps where you can see big swaths of sky. The trail may be underneath this open dome.

Finally, look at the surface of the snow in the direction the trail ought to go. Is there a depression where other skiers or snowshoers may have compacted the snow? Is the snow firm underfoot but soft off to the sides? If so, you're probably on the trail.

Losing the trail happens any number of times on a mountain trip, but normally the group finds the path within minutes. As long as everyone keeps track of the terrain, trail finding can be a game, not a cause for panic.

Low Visibility

Heavy, wind-driven snowstorms that obliterate all natural landmarks or opaque skies that diminish depth perception and induce vertigo are both common in the mountains. One day in February, in New Hampshire's Presidential Range, we experienced heavy snow driven by 50-mile-per-hour winds that erased the features of the summit ridge. This is a region with such a harsh climate that only tiny plants, grasses, and weather-blasted rock survive there. Compounding the visibility problem, my goggles were completely fogged.

"Damn, it's thick out here," I thought as I stumbled ahead through the white chaos. Just then, Joe Lentini leaned over and, fighting the roar of the wind, screamed in my ear.

"You know, it's crazy, but I love this stuff!"

A shadow appeared out of the gloom. A rock cairn! I tapped it with my ski pole, just to make sure, mumbled a thank you under my breath, and felt my way toward the next one.

In this case, even though we couldn't see more than a dozen yards or so, we knew which way we were traveling (south) because the wind, which was blowing furiously from the west, was striking the right side of our faces, arms, and legs. There was little chance of getting turned around with such an unerring guide, so we concentrated on trying to remain upright moving from cairn to cairn.

At times, when you can't even see the next cairn—indeed, at times when you can't see your hand in front of your face—you may have to rope up. One person should stand at the cairn while another, attached to the first person with a rope, searches for the next cairn. Progress will be slow, but it will also be sure, and you won't become separated. Climbing rope— 120 feet or so of 8-millimeter rope—can come in handy at times like this.

When you can't see and there are no cairns, consider finding a sheltered spot out of the wind, bundling up in your warm clothes, having something to eat, and waiting for visibility to improve. If you must continue, make sure members of the group stay together and follow a compass bearing until you get to a safe place. Be careful; even experienced mountaineers have walked off cliffs in poor light conditions.

Avalanches

Avalanches occur wherever there are snow-covered slopes. When the conditions are favorable, snow will slide. Every winter traveler should have some basic familiarity with avalanches, their causes, and how to avoid them.

In simplest terms, an avalanche is a mass of snow sliding down a slope at anywhere from trotting speed to over 100 miles per hour. Along the way, avalanches often pick up riders—brush, boulders, trees, and sometimes an unwary wilderness traveler. Anyone who witnesses the awesome power generated by tons of falling snow will not soon forget the spectacle.

Steve Barnett considers avalanches "the single greatest problem facing the ski tourer. . . . Too often you can step into mortal danger without realizing that anything is wrong. In fact, it's often the most alluring slopes and conditions—open bowls full of fresh deep powder, for example—that present the greatest hazards."

But it's not just backcountry skiers and riders who are at risk. Hikers, climbers, snowmobilers, and snowshoers must also be aware of the danger posed by snow-covered slopes.

There are two basic types of avalanches: (1) loose-snow avalanches, which originate at a single point and fan out, incorporating more and more unconsolidated snow as they travel down the slope; and (2) slab avalanches, which occur when a massive block of cohesive snow cracks off a slope and begins to slide.

Loose-snow avalanches often occur during or just after periods of heavy snowfall, when the accumulated weight of the new-fallen snow succumbs to the forces of gravity and slides off the slope. The basic ingredients of a loose-snow avalanche include a slope of 25 degrees or greater; snowfall of 1 inch or more per hour or 10 to 12 inches or more total accumulation; and a surface for the snow to slide upon, such as a loose layer of round depth-hoar crystals or a snow surface smoothed by freeze, rain, or thaw action.

Slab avalanches occur when well-compacted and cohesive snow layers are not securely anchored to a slope. If there's a weak layer of snow without cohesion, melt water, or crust beneath the compact layer, the slope is primed to avalanche. All that's needed to release the slab and send it crashing down is a trigger mechanism. A skier or snowshoer may unwittingly provide that mechanism by crossing the release zone, or area at the top of the slide where the fracture occurs, thereby triggering the avalanche.

Traveling in Avalanche Country

The only way to travel in avalanche country and survive is to minimize the risks involved. Be aware of your surroundings—constantly look, listen, feel, and evaluate. Be extremely vigilant when crossing danger zones, and if the snowpack appears unstable, heed Colorado backcountry skier Lou Dawson's advice to "be cautious and conservative to the point of absurdity" when planning your route or when deciding to ski an inviting slope.

Plan to travel on the ridge tops or in heavily wooded areas as much as possible. Load any slopes with as few people as possible; make sure

An avalanche in motion. *Photograph courtesy of Richard Armstrong, National Snow and Ice Data Center.*

your group is spread out over the slope. Keep each other in sight at all times. Never travel above your partners, and never stop in the middle of steep slopes.

If the snowpack is suspect, always ascend summits via the ridgelines and make the descent using the exact same route. Stay far back from overhanging cornices. Avoid the midslopes and the release zone near the top of the slope. Most victims actually trigger the avalanche that buries them. Avoiding a suspected slope by detouring completely above or below it significantly reduces the danger. Other dangerous places to travel are in gullies or at the base of steep open slopes.

As you travel, always keep an eye on the slopes around you. Remember that the vast majority (more than 40 percent) of avalanches occur on slopes with a steepness of between 30 and 45 degrees—exactly where expert skiers want to be. Also, even if you are on a slope with a lesser angle, always check the slope above you. Many skiers have been caught by slides that release above them—sometimes at quite a distance.

Whenever you're in the mountains, constantly be on the lookout for evidence of sliding-avalanche chutes, cracks in the snowpack where slabs have broken off, point releases around rocky outcrops, or slide paths where the timber has literally been torn away.

Look at the slopes around you for signs of snow sloughs, or small slides, indicating the potential presence of avalanche danger. Finally, keep track of the weather as you proceed. The first 24-hour period after a heavy snowfall, high wind, rain, or thaw is the most dangerous. Slopes may remain dangerous for very long periods of time if heavy snow occurs in cold temperatures. In milder weather, waiting a day or more after an avalanche-promoting weather event significantly reduces the danger. Snow falling during the high winds of a blizzard is apt to form a dangerous slab layer. Also, avoid new snow falling

Snow School

Why is snow white?

According to the National Snow and Ice Data Center, "[V]isible sunlight is white. Most natural materials absorb some sunlight, which gives them their color. Snow, however, reflects most of the sunlight. The complex structure of snow crystals results in countless tiny surfaces from which visible light is efficiently reflected. What little sunlight is absorbed by snow is absorbed uniformly over the wavelengths of visible light, thus giving snow its white appearance." •

A clinometer is a very useful tool for measuring the angel of a slope. Most avalanches occur on slopes between 30 and 45 degrees. *Photograph courtesy of Brunton.*

on smooth, rain-crusted, or sun-crusted snow.

If you must cross a danger zone, gather as much information about the snowpack as possible to determine whether avalanche conditions prevail. One way to do this is to use your ski pole to probe the snow. Push the pole into the snow whenever you're on suspect terrain. If the pole encounters smooth, even resistance, there is less likelihood that the slope will slide. If the pole encounters uneven resistance—if it breaks through a buried layer of crust or punches from compact snow into loose layers of unconsolidated snow—the slope is potentially unstable and is more likely to avalanche.

A better way to gather information about the snowpack is to dig a test pit in the snow. By exposing a cross section of the snowpack, you can examine the different layers and check for weaknesses. For instance, if you locate a hard crust supporting a foot of consolidated snow, head elsewhere because that top layer might very well be a slab avalanche waiting for a trigger. Likewise, if you dig down and uncover layers of snow characterized by coarse, grainy snow crystals, the slope is probably not safe, whereas if all the layers are firm and well bonded, it might be safer. When digging your pit, choose a safe location on an adjacent slope that is similar in exposure, aspect, and steepness to the suspect one.

If the decision is made to cross the slope, remove your ski pole straps and undo all pack buckles so you can quickly free yourself from your gear if you need to. Put on additional warm clothing to ward off the chill in case you're trapped, and zip up your parka and fasten all your clothing securely to keep snow from entering through cuffs, collars, or other openings. Make sure your electronic avalanche beacons are turned on to "transmit," are in good working order, and are securely fastened.

Take a look at the slope you're about to cross. Are there any islands of safety such as very large rock outcrops or stands of trees that you can head to as you cross? If so, plan your route to take advantage of whatever security these natural features have to offer. Race to these islands of safety or the sides of the slope as quickly as possible if the snow starts to slide.

Digging a test pit allows you to see potential avalanche dangers in the exposed cross section of snow.

You must cross the slope one at a time. The others should watch from a position where they can see the whole slope. If the person crossing is caught in a slide, the others can locate the position where the victim was last seen. Searching should begin immediately below that point.

One last important piece of advice comes from Doug Fesler, founder and director of the Alaska Mountain Safety Center, who once told me to "always make sure you have a woman in your party, and listen to her. Women are a lot more comfortable saying no and turning around if the situation is unsafe than guys are."

A test pit can reveal, for instance, layers of slab snow resting on dangerous layers of depth hoar—an avalanche just waiting for a trigger such as a skier or snowboarder.

Everyone in the group should carry an avalanche shovel, a beacon, and probe.

Avalanche Rescue

As soon as a victim knows he's caught in a slide, he must act quickly to help ensure his own survival. There are several steps he can take to self-rescue.

1. When he realizes he's caught in a slide, the victim should yell to alert companions.

2. The victim should try to jettison his pack and head quickly to an island of safety.

3. If this is not possible, the victim should try to stay above the snow by making swimming motions.

4. Before the snow stops moving, the victim should try to make an air pocket by punching out the snow in front of his nose and mouth,

and then he should take a deep breath to expand the snow around the chest.

5. The victim should also try to reach a hand through to the surface above him.

6. If he can, the victim should try to dig himself out.

As soon as the slope is settled and there are no indications of further avalanching, the other members of the group must take action quickly to rescue the victim. Speed is of the essence: A victim's chances of survival diminishes to only 50 percent after the first half hour. What the group does in the next few minutes is critical. It's wise to rehearse actions in advance.

1. The rescuers should closely watch the victim's path as he's caught in the slide.

2. All rescuers must then immediately switch their beacons to "receive."

3. With ski poles, packs, or other highly visible objects, rescuers should mark where the avalanche (point A) first struck the victim and where he was last seen (point B).

4. The rescuers must then visualize a line between points A and B. This is the path in which the victim was swept. A quick search should be made directly below point B. Any clues—hat, gloves, ski poles, and so forth—should be well marked.

5. If the quick search fails to reveal the victim immediately, the rescuers must begin a transceiver (beacon) search right way. All transceivers use exactly the same frequency, but not all models work the same way, so it's very important to read your instruction manual and practice ahead of time in order to pinpoint the victim's location as quickly as possible.

6. Once you've zeroed in on

Snow School

What is the typical profile of an avalanche victim?

According to the Colorado Avalanche Information Center, 89 percent of avalanche victims in the United States are male, most are between the ages of 20 and 29, and 75 percent are experienced backcountry travelers. •

the victim's location, start probing the immediate area until you actually locate him beneath the snow.

7. As soon as the victim is located, he must be uncovered. Sturdy shovels are required for this task, and any individual traveling in the mountains should bring one along.

8. Once uncovered, the victim should be treated for shock, hypothermia, frostbite, fractures, and any other injuries incurred during the slide. Because head and neck injuries are common, be especially careful when moving avalanche victims.

The United States Avalanche Danger Scale

Danger Level	Avalanche Probability and Avalanche Trigger	Degree and Distribution of Avalanche Danger	Recommended Actions in the Backcountry
Low	Natural and human-triggered avalanches are very unlikely.	Snow is generally stable, with isolated areas of instability.	Travel is generally safe. Normal caution is advised.
Moderate	Natural avalanches are unlikely; human-triggered avalanches are possible.	Unstable slabs are possible on steep terrain.	Use caution on steeper terrain on certain aspects.
Considerable	Natural avalanches are possible; human-triggered avalanches are probable.	Unstable slabs are probable on steep terrain.	Use increasing caution on steeper terrain.
High	Natural and human-triggered avalanches are likely.	Unstable slabs are likely on a variety of aspects and slope angles.	Travel in avalanche terrain is not recommended; travel is safest on windward ridges of low-angle slopes without steep terrain above.
Extreme	Widespread natural and human-triggered avalanches are certain.	Extremely unstable slabs are certain on most aspects and slope angles. Large, destructive avalanches are possible.	Avoid all travel in avalanche terrain; travel should be confined to low-angle terrain well away from avalanche path run-outs.

Winterlude: The Professional Approach

In 1913, the great American explorer Vilhjalmur Steffanson ventured out onto the drifting pack ice north of the Alaska coast with only minimal supplies. His goal was to explore one of the last great blank spaces on the map, and he wanted to prove that with the proper skills and training, people could survive in what was considered an uninhabitable desert of ice.

Soon after he set out, Steffanson was given up for dead. Search parties were sent, and the rescuers never returned—but Steffanson did. Upon completion of his expedition several years later, a reporter asked him if he had any "adventures." "Nope," Steffanson replied, "No adventures. Just experiences. Adventure is the result of incompetence."

By using his skills and a few well-chosen tools, Steffanson thrived on local resources where others thought life was unsustainable. Steffanson not only endured, but he also applied himself to the study of his environment—ice, wind, waves, weather, and animals—and to the practice of critical travel and survival skills. His diligence paid off: He learned to maximize the benefits and minimize the hardships of his surroundings.

Chapter 12

In Camp

I t's midafternoon and already you feel as though you've put in a long
day. Yet there's a lot of work to be done. You glance at the sun to estimate how much daylight remains: Looks like there's about an hour left. To
be more precise in your measurement, you take off your glove, extend your
arm, and, keeping together your four fingers (not the thumb), you measure
the distance from the bottom of the sun to the top of the horizon. There's
an even four fingers in width, which translates into about an hour of direct
light and maybe another half hour of twilight. Time to set up camp.

Choosing a Campsite

Sometimes ideal campsites are hard to find, and after a hard day, almost any
place can feel like a room at the Ritz. Yet if you plan ahead and actually
make camping a priority on your winter camping trip, you can spend the
night in some fine places. Here are a few qualities to keep an eye out for.

• **Scenery.** After all, you're on this trip to enjoy yourselves, and views are
a big part of why you came. Views of surrounding peaks, lakes, or forests
add immeasurably to your camping experience. Before you set up your
tent, however, bear in mind wind, avalanche risk, cold-air drainage, exposure, water availability, and whether the ground is level.

• **Wind.** Be sure your tents won't blow away if the wind starts howling.
Campsites on ridges are spectacular, but they're also very exposed. Trees,
large rock outcrops, blowdowns, and other features provide shelter. You
can judge the wind direction and find shelter in the lee side. Also, be
aware that wind can blow down dead trees and widow makers (trees that
are already toppled but are hung up in the branches of other trees) that
are just waiting for a strong gust to send them crashing. Always look up
when you scout a potential campsite.

This delightful winter campsite has good views, is sheltered, and is safe from avalanche run-outs.

- **Avalanche risk.** Having an avalanche slam into your campsite would certainly be a rude awakening. Be sure to stay away from potential avalanche slopes, and before you set up for the night, check to make sure you're far, far away from any avalanche path.
- **Cold-air drainage.** Remember that cold air sinks, so if you camp at the bottom of a valley, your campsite will be much colder than one slightly higher up. Only a few feet in elevation can make an enormous difference.
- **Exposure.** Facing south will give you longer days and more direct sunlight. A north-facing camp will, of course, provide just the opposite.
- **Water.** Having a source of water close by will save lots of time and fuel spent melting snow. Swift streams often remain unfrozen throughout the winter. If the sources are frozen over, you can usually cut through the ice with a hatchet or an ice ax to reach water. If the water source is frozen solid, remember that melted ice provides more water than melted snow.
- **Level ground.** A level site is always desirable. If the terrain is uncooperative, flatten out the snow to create a level site or dig tent sites out of the snowpack with your shovels. As we will see, one of the best parts about winter camping is snow—it's a great building material. What you can create out of it is limited only by your imagination.

Of course, you can hope that all your campsites will be sheltered from the wind and near water and on level ground and have excellent views. Don't count on it, but remember you can almost always locate potential campsites in advance by checking your map. When you get to a promising area, drop your packs and scout around for the best possible site. When you agree on a location, it's time to get to work.

Setting up Camp

Once you've decided to set up camp, the group members must divide the tasks and share the work. At a typical winter tent camp, the tasks that need immediate attention include erecting tents, building a kitchen area, collecting firewood, and getting water.

Erecting Tents

With your skis, split board, or snowshoes, pack the entire area of the campsite, especially where the tents will be set up, so the snow is compressed. Doing this hardens the snow, making it easy to walk around the camp area without sinking down into the snow (called post holing). If you don't pack the snow, you'll have a hard time moving around the campsite.

Then erect the tents with the doors toward the central area, where the kitchen is going to be located. If there's a strong wind blowing, turn the tents so the doors are at a right angle to the wind.

Tent stakes are basically extra weight in winter, so use your skis, poles, ice axes, or fallen branches as stakes. Or, to provide extra stability and security, stake your tent with what's known as a dead man. To make a dead man, tie the stake line to a stick, scoop out a hole in the snow, and bury the stick. Compress the snow over the buried stick and allow it to settle. Soon the snow will harden around the dead man like a concrete overcoat.

If, despite your best efforts, the wind continues to tug at your tent, get out your shovels and build a wall around the tent to protect it from the wind. Make the wall as high as necessary. Have someone inside the tent push the snow away from the tent walls so they don't collapse. Pack the snow so that when it hardens, you'll have a wall of extra insulation 6 to 12 inches thick all the way around the bottom half of the tent, making it extra cozy on even the coldest night.

Eskimos in northern Labrador cut snow blocks to protect their tent from the cold wind.

To add to the comfort of your living quarters, dig a rectangular pit a couple of feet deep in front of your tent. This makes it easier to take off your boots in the evening and put them on again in the morning—and you'll appreciate not always having to sit with your legs stretched straight out or crossed.

Finally, when your tent is erect, toss in your sleeping pads and sleeping bags. The bags will air out and regain their fluffiness while you take care of other chores. As a last touch, hang a candle lantern from the tent ceiling to use when you're ready for bed. It's nice to have some light when you get ready for sleep, and a candle lantern will save flashlight batteries.

Building the Kitchen Area

Meanwhile, as the tents are going up, one or two people can start building the kitchen area—the place where you'll cook, eat, relax, warm up, repair your equipment, and plan the next day's adventures. The kitchen area is the community center of a winter camp.

Get the shovels and start digging out a round pit, or kiva, as a friend calls it, in the snow. The kiva should be at least 6 to 8 feet in diameter for a group of 4 to 6 people and larger for a bigger group.

As you dig from the inside of the circle, pile the snow around the sides of the pit. When you've excavated a flat-bottomed crater 2 or 3 feet deep, there will be a mound of snow all the way around. Pack this snow with your shovel until it's firm.

Then, either carve benches in the snow for people to sit on or jump into the mounded snow seat first to create perfect, anatomically correct lounge chairs. In no time these contoured seats will set up firmly and be ready for you to relax and enjoy the evening. Finally, stick snowshoes or skis upright into the snow behind the chairs to serve as backrests. Total decadence!

The rest of the snow around the kiva can now be carved into tables, shelves, and counters for the cook to use. If you're using a stove, carve out a windproof place for the stove and storage places for food and utensils. Having the stove, food, and cooking equipment at waist or chest level is a real treat because you don't have to do all the cooking bent over or kneeling down. Make yourself at home.

The fire should be built in the center of the kiva. The cook will benefit from the warmth, and the rest of the group can bask in the heat, lounge around on the snow benches, and relax. Even on a bitterly cold

A well-appointed campsite—including a fire at the center of the kiva and carved seats on the perimeter of the pit—makes a winter camping trip warm, cozy, and comfortable.

night, the snow walls around the kiva reflect an enormous amount of heat. It's only when you get up and move away from the fire that you realize how cold the temperature is.

Building the Fire

Campfires are a topic of controversy—and for good reason. If you go to the local state or provincial park, you can see the blackened areas where the ground has been charred and every tree has been hacked and stripped. Bits of partially burned foil, beer cans, and half-burned logs are scattered about. Clearly, a lot of people don't know how to make a proper campfire, and the environment suffers.

Yet to suggest that fires are categorically unsound and environmentally degrading is not true. On long trips in frigid places such as interior Alaska or Labrador, they're essential. There's a skill to building a safe, efficient fire that burns hot, doesn't smoke, and leaves no trace to mar the next person's outdoor experience. Fire building is like any other winter camping skill—expertise comes with awareness, patient attention to detail, and practice. It can be done.

Care should be used in the selection of firewood, not only to preserve the integrity of the site but also to ensure the best possible fire. Scout the areas away from your campsite for small diameter (3- to 4-inch) standing or leaning dead trees with hard, dry wood. If you can find one with the bark gone, so much the better—it's the moisture trapped by the bark that causes a fire to smoke. Of course, wet wood will smoke too, so make sure your tree is dry.

A tree this size is unlikely to be a residence for birds or small mammals, but check anyway. When you're sure the tree is uninhabited, saw it off at the base right at ground level so the cut won't be noticeable to a sharp eye. Use your hatchet to remove any branches, and gather these for kindling. Cut the tree into 12- to 14-inch sections with your saw, and then split these sections into quarters with your ax. You should have an armful or two of thin, even-length strips of firewood—perfect material for cooking because of the clean, even heat it produces and because you can easily adjust the flame by adding just the right number of sticks to the fire. Good-quality firewood prepared in this manner is consumed completely, leaving no partially burned remains and no coals, just a layer of very fine ash.

Before you start your fire, collect all your fire-starting materials. You'll need tinder to start the flame, small kindling to feed it while it grows, and larger wood to burn for cooking, heat, and light.

Tinder can be a strip of birch bark taken from a dead tree or picked up from the ground. I collect dead birch bark and usually have a small sack of it for starting fires. Dried grasses, dead pine needles, or very dry, matchstick-thin sticks collected from blowdowns or dead branches also work well. Kindling can be very finely split, pencil-thin pieces of firewood, and of course, your burning wood comes from a standing dead tree, as described earlier. Place tinder, kindling, and firewood in separate piles where they won't be in the way of other camp activity.

Before you begin to build your fire, consider how you'll keep it from melting the snow and sinking out of sight. Also, if you've dug down to ground level, how will you keep the fire from scorching and scarring the forest floor? The answer to both considerations is insulation. If you dig down to the ground, your fire won't sink but it may harm the soil—and you don't want to do that. Instead, a thick platform of dead branches provides insulation. Find some thick, dead wood—rotting logs, old stump wood, or other forest litter—and build a platform in the center of the fire pit.

For added insulation and even more ground protection, some winter campers build their fires on small metal trash can lids, metal trays, or cookie sheets. These metal sheets, placed atop a layer of dead wood, collect all the ashes and insulate the ground from the fire, leaving absolutely no sign that a fire was ever built there.

At this point, you have a fire kiva that's about 8 feet across—wide enough to permit a good draft and provide the fire with plenty of air—and you have bone-dry tinder, kindling, and firewood. (Remember, wet wood won't burn unless you shave it paper thin.) You also have a match. You're almost ready.

Place your tinder on the platform and lean a few tiny, dry pieces of kindling against it. Now light the tinder. As it springs into flame, slowly feed more kindling onto the fire. Make sure that you leave plenty of air space between the sticks of kindling and don't smother the young flame. Let it grow in size and strength, feeding it carefully all the while. Be patient. When the flame has gathered enough strength, start using bigger pieces of kindling until the fire is able to accept your split lengths of firewood. You should now have a hot, bright, smokeless fire—without degrading the environment.

A word about matches: I use the strike-anywhere kind, keep them in waterproof containers, and have them stashed all over the place—in the first aid kit; in my possibles sack, where I keep all my important odds and ends; and in the pockets of my parka and wind shell. You can bring along butane lighters as well or in place of matches, but remember that butane will not light in extremely cold weather unless you keep it warm. If you do bring a lighter, wear it on a parachute-cord necklace under your shirt, where it will always stay warm enough to use.

Getting Water

Unfortunately, many once-pure water supplies must now be regarded with suspicion. That we now assume that water supplies will be unhealthy

Build a fire on a raft of wood to keep it from sinking into the snow.

speaks volumes on how distant we are from nature and how badly we've abused our planet. Poisoned water is now the norm, not the exception, in all but the most remote wilderness locations. What should you do?

Leave the water filtration system at home; it will quickly freeze into a useless block of ice and plastic. Water purification tablets or iodine drops aren't as much use as they are in the summer, either: Their effectiveness is temperature related, and they don't work very well in the cold. The purification method of choice in winter is to bring water to a rolling boil.

Getting enough water is much easier if you're near a stream or lake. Your map will indicate likely sources of water. If you can find a source of open water, you're in luck. If not, cut through the ice with your ax or ice ax until you find water. Some northern travelers who know that every night they'll have to cut through 2 or 3 feet of ice to get to water bring along a long-handled harpoonlike ice chisel to expedite the process. When you cut a hole in the ice, be sure to mark it clearly with something visible—a ski, a snowshoe, an evergreen bough—so no one trips in the hole

When you're getting water, use an ice chisel to chip through thick lake ice.

and so you can find it easily in a storm. If the hole is deep, tie a string to your water bottle and lower it down into the hole with your ski pole.

When you melt snow, save a swallow or two from your water bottle and put it in the pot with the snow. The moisture will speed up the boiling process and will keep your pot from scorching. Pack as much snow as you can into the pot and keep adding it as more and more snow melts. For melting, keep snow blocks or, even better, chunks of ice, handy near the stove.

Getting Comfortable

You've succeeded at creating a typical winter tent camp. It's now dark, and up to this time you've been running around keeping busy. But with the work done, you're starting to cool off. Time to get out of your trail clothes and into nice dry evening wear.

Before you become chilled, take off wet clothes and put on dry ones. Some people change into a soft, synthetic turtleneck, dry socks, pile or wool pants, and fiberfill booties. A pair of pack-cloth mukluks over the booties protects the booties from moisture, allowing you to wander around the camp area without worrying about getting them wet. Bring your wet clothes to the fire and set up a drying rack. One of the wonderful things about a campfire is that it can dry your wet items every night. Just be sure not to put any clothing items close to the fire; you should determine how close you can comfortably hold your hands to the flames and make certain the clothes go no closer than this to avoid having some pretty crispy clothes.

Now kick back in your snow-sculpted lounge chair, bask in the hypnotic warmth of the fire, have a hot drink, make some popcorn, watch the flames leap and dance, and keep the cooks company.

Cooking

You can cook over the fire or on a stove. To cook over the fire, you need to be able to suspend the pots over the flames. Easy enough: Just cut a long wooden pole, stick it deep into the snow bank or the snow next to the fire so that it stretches above the flames, and hang your pots from it. Or cut some wood into three even lengths about 4 feet long each, lash them together at the top, and use this tripod to hang your pot.

Another way to suspend pots is to hammer sharpened sticks (with the hammer side of the ax head) upright in the snow on either side of the fire, then place another stick above the fire and lash it to the upright sticks. You can use this spit to hang pots directly over the flames. Wire works well, but best of all are small chains (available at hardware stores) with S hooks. You can use the S hooks to raise or lower your pots in order to regulate the heat. The thin pieces of split wood used for cooking also give you great control over the amount of heat the fire gives to pots.

When cooking with a camp stove, remember to refuel the stove away from the fire and away from where you plan to use it. To prevent combustion, store all your stove fuel away from the cooking area. Also, never light the stove where you fill it, since any fuel you spill might catch fire.

To keep the stove from sinking into the snow, place underneath the stove a metal sheet, such as a cookie sheet, a license plate, or a metal shovel blade. Remember, too, that wind is the natural enemy of stove efficiency. You can use a windscreen or place snow blocks upwind to shield the stove.

Always start with a full tank of fuel, but if you run out in the middle of your meal, let the stove cool off before you try to refill it. At the end of the meal, let the stove cool, and then refill it so it will be ready to go at a moment's notice.

Start the meal by heating water for hot drinks or soups and keep them coming. Hot drinks are a great way to replace body fluids lost during the day, and just holding a steaming mug makes people feel warm and cozy.

When everyone has his or her hot drink, prepare the main meal. The meals described in chapter 8 are all of the one-pot variety, so there should be little confusion. Just add the ingredients to the pot of boiling water, and add a tablespoon or two of butter or margarine to everything to help keep you warm while you sleep.

Sanitation

A fresh coat of snow makes the world look brand new. In the spring, however, when it melts, the ugliness of poor camping practices is revealed: Half-burned logs and bits of charred sticks are everywhere. Plastic bags and twist ties lie scattered about. Toilet paper degrades the scene and fouls the water supply. And local animals, accustomed to associating humans with food scraps, approach boldly, waiting for a handout. If they don't get one—and especially if they do—they'll chew through your expensive camping equipment to get at your food supply.

To avoid creating another such place, try to leave each campsite as clean or cleaner than you found it. Pack out everything you bring in, down to the last scrap of foil from a ski wax canister. Every time you cook an evening meal, you'll have empty plastic bags. You can use these to pack out your trash.

To relieve yourself, go some distance from camp (alerting someone in the group that you're "going for a walk"). Be sure to choose a site that's far away from any water source and is well off trail, away from areas of activity.

Some people choose to forego the use of toilet paper, using natural materials available close at hand. If you choose to use paper, however, be sure to burn it completely or pack it out. Disguise the area and accelerate the decomposition process by covering the waste with rotting stumps, sticks, or other forest detritus.

Food scraps can either be burned in a hot fire until they're completely consumed or packed out.

You can clean up the fire area by burning wood completely and by picking up your ash-filled lid or metal sheet and scattering the ashes over a broad area far away from camp, trail, or anywhere anyone is likely to go.

Believe it or not, it's entirely possible to keep clean and wash up on the winter trail. Most of us are more comfortable and sleep better if we regularly rinse off the sweat and grime we've accumulated during our efforts. All you need to do is take a bucket bath: Simply warm a large pot of water on the stove or the fire, strip down and stand on your shorty pad, and pour some of that wonderful warm water over your head. When you've finished lathering up, rinse off with the rest of the water. It's easy and takes very little time to keep clean.

Sleeping Warmly

After dinner, chances are you'll want to relax around the fire for a while, sipping hot drinks, making popcorn, perhaps telling stories or reliving the highlights of the day. First, though, it's a good idea to fill all the water bottles with warm water so there'll be plenty for the morning. You can also bring these into your sleeping bag with you. The extra warmth will feel good, and they won't freeze overnight. Finally, before you hit the sack, put away everything—stoves, food bags, cups and utensils, and so forth. If you don't and you get a foot of snow overnight, you'll spend the next day digging around for important items. Think ahead.

Most folks don't hang food in winter unless they suspect bear activity. In winter, bears are probably hibernating. In late fall, late winter, or during a thaw, however, bears may become active—and chances are they'll be hungry. At these times, use your rope and string up the food. Here's an easy, step-by-step way to do this.

1. Start with a length of rope. To one end tie a small, heavy object.

2. Find two trees approximately 20 feet apart and about 100 yards or so downwind from your camp. Throw the weighted end of the rope over a limb of the first tree, some 15 feet off the ground.

3. Remove the weight and tie the end of the rope to the trunk of the first tree.

4. Tie the small, heavy object to the other end of the rope, and toss this end over a limb of the second tree, about 15 feet off the ground.

5. Attach your food bags to the center of the rope. A carabiner is useful for this purpose.

6. Pull on the second end of the rope and hoist the food bags into the air, making sure they're 12 feet or more above the surface of the snow. Tie the second end of the rope to the second tree trunk.

7. If you have reason to suspect bears are active, do your cooking where you'll hang your food—roughly 100 yards downwind from the camp.

When all the chores have been finished, sit down, relax, tilt your head back, and gaze overhead through the trees at the billions of stars dancing overhead, looking closer than ever. Perhaps a coyote or, in the far north, a wolf, will begin to sing. Its presence lends a feeling of power and mystery to the winter wilderness.

Before long, a pleasant weariness will overcome you, and you'll start to think about sleep. It's much easier if tent mates get settled one at a time. Each person has to undress and dress and arrange clothing, sleeping bags, and sleeping pads, and in a cramped tent, getting settled can be awkward if everyone tries to organize sleeping at once. It's best to take turns.

Getting a good night's sleep on the winter trail is a real skill. There are several steps you can take to stay warm and comfortable all night long.

First, wear plenty of clothes to bed. Forget that nonsense about sleeping warmer with fewer clothes on. The person who said that never spent a –30-degree night in a sleeping bag. The more insulation you're wearing, the better. Sleep fully dressed, including a hat or balaclava, pile jacket, and Polarguard booties if necessary. If you get too hot, you can always remove a layer!

Remember that you lose most of your heat through your head and neck, so wear a neck warmer or wrap a sweater around your neck like a shawl. Try to plug any gaps in the insulation around your neck and face, keeping in the warm air and keeping out the cold air. Try to keep your nose and mouth outside the bag; when you breathe inside the sleeping bag and exhale moist air, you create a damp, clammy atmosphere. If your nose is getting nipped, put on your face mask.

When you get into your bag, create a small depression in the snow beneath it for your hips and buttocks. You'll be much more comfortable. Also, remember that you can lose a tremendous amount of heat through conduction to the cold snow beneath your tent, so put any extra clothing beneath you. Make sure your sleeping pads are inflated and positioned correctly. If you roll off them during the night, you'll soon know it.

Don't get into your sleeping bag when you're cold. Remember, the bag is only insulation, it doesn't generate heat—you do that. If you get into your bag after a quick jog around the camp, running in place, or doing jumping jacks, you'll warm up your bag much faster.

Nibbling on food during the night provides extra energy to keep you warm, so be sure to keep some handy. If you wake up cold, eat a handful of gorp or some other high-energy food right away.

Use the buddy system and sleep bundled up next to your partners. Borrow some of their body heat—after all, what are friends for?

If you're still cold after all this, get a new sleeping bag with more loft before your next trip.

Finally, it happens to everybody: In the middle of the night you suddenly realize you have to relieve yourself. Oh, no! "It's cold out there," you may say, "Forget it!" But then you start getting colder because your body is keeping all that excess fluid warm—and you can't get back to sleep. Bite the bullet and do it! It takes only a few seconds, and it sure beats lying awake half the night.

Some winter campers bring a specially designated (and well-marked) pee bottle into the tent for just such occasions. Others use a can, which is more convenient for women. (Just don't knock it over.)

Finally, think about tomorrow. Unless you want a pair of iceboxes for your feet, you'll have to do something about your boot liners. The only way they'll stay warm is if you put them at the bottom of your sleeping bag at night or wear them on your feet. Pleasant dreams!

Snow Shelters

While tents are generally more convenient, easier to use, and faster to set up, knowing how to build a snow shelter in an emergency can save your life. Snow shelters can also be a lot of fun to build, and if you're going to make a base camp for a few days, they can be quite luxurious.

There are advantages to living in snow shelters. For one, they're very warm. On a night when the mercury has shriveled into a little ball at the bottom of the thermometer (real bragging cold), the temperature will be at or just above freezing inside a snow shelter. For another, when the wind is howling and perhaps tearing down tents (it does happen), inside the snow shelter all's quiet, peaceful, and calm so that you can soon forget there's a storm raging outside.

Finally, with a little imagination a shelter allows you to design your own ideal living space—with shelves here and storage compartments there. And when you light your candle lantern, the ice crystals reflect the light, bouncing it off the domed interior to create a bright, cheerful atmosphere.

If you build a snow shelter, just remember to put on your shell garments. You can get wet digging around in all that snow.

Because igloos require a firm slab snow that isn't commonly found outside vast, windswept areas such as the Canadian Barrens, I'll leave discussion of their construction to someone else and instead discuss two types of snow shelters that are easy to build wherever it snows.

Snow Caves

The snow cave is perhaps the easiest snow shelter to build—all you need is a minimum of 5 or 6 feet of drifted snow and something to use for digging. You can use pots, snowshoes, even your hands if you're desperate, but a couple of shovels will make the work go much faster.

Snow collects in deep drifts on the leeward side of fallen trees, boulders, and ridges. Lee slopes along stream banks can be ideal spots for a snow cave. Physical obstruction creates an eddy in the air currents, and the snow tends to pile up behind whatever is creating the eddy. So when you're scouting around for a likely snow cave location, start by probing the drifts on leeward slopes.

When you find a likely spot, start digging. Make an entrance about 3 feet high by 3 feet wide. Dig straight into the leeward slope, and then start angling the entrance tunnel upward. A rising entrance allows the cold air to sink out of the cave.

When the entrance tunnel is done, start digging out the main chamber of the cave. The interior should have a domed ceiling—a shape that's tremendously strong and most unlikely to collapse. Make the room as big as you like or, if you're digging in a small drift, as big as you can. Just be sure the roof is at least 12 inches thick. You can check this as you dig by thrusting a sharp stick upward through the snow. Have someone outside let you know when the stick emerges and then estimate how much of the stick is submerged in snow.

Work in tandem with another person who's at the entrance of the snow cave, shoveling away all the snow rubble from the excavation going on inside. When you get going, the snow can really start to fly, so take a break now and then and trade positions. It can be hot and stuffy when you work on the inside.

When you're done with snow removal, for ventilation, poke a hole the size of a small fist through the dome. Now you can start working on the interior touches.

Remember to leave your skis or snowshoes at the entrance to the cave so it can be located in the dark or if it's snowing. Keep a shovel inside the cave in case you have to dig your way out in the morning. Finally, for additional warmth, put your packs in the entrance and block off the door.

The Athabaskan Snow House

Building an Athabaskan snow house, or quinzhee, as the Athabaskan Indians call it, is an ingenious way to make a snow cave when there are no deep drifts readily available. To build a quinzhee, all you need is snow and a shovel. You can even build one just using a snowshoe for a shovel if you have to. Unlike an igloo, a quinzhee doesn't require the hard slab snow of tundra regions and is much easier to make. The quinzhee can be built wherever there's loose snow on the ground.

To build a comfortable two- to three-person quinzhee, measure a circle about 7 feet in diameter. When you have drawn the perimeter of the quinzhee, start shoveling loose snow into the circle, piling it up until the top of the mound is about 6 feet or so above the ground.

Let the snow set up for about an hour. (Depending upon the consistency of the snow, this takes more or less time: more for powder, less for heavy snow.) Then start digging out the living space as though it were a snow cave. Carve out a domed ceiling, punch an air hole, and make the entrance slightly lower than the main chamber to expedite cold air seepage. Once you block the door with your packs, you're set for the night. Let the storms howl outside! You won't even know it.

Inside the snow shelter, you can carve shelves for your personal items or for candles and customize the interior any way you like. Place a ground sheet on the snow, and then place your sleeping pads on this. Make yourself at home as you would in your tent.

Morning on the Winter Trail

I'm often the first one up in the morning, a habit that surfaces only on camping trips and lies dormant the rest of the year. Maybe the fresh air and the anticipation of all the good skiing and snowshoeing to come wakens me. Whatever the cause, as the first one up, I volunteer for a lot of work nobody else wants to do.

That's all right, though. Mornings are often the best part of the day. It's nice to get going slowly in the earliest pale light and watch the frozen world come alive. There's no rush; it's just you and a cold winter morning, offering a peaceful solitude, a communion that few people are lucky enough to experience.

First, after checking the thermometer for the overnight low temperature (bragging rights!), I get a fire going, put on some hot water, and enjoy the first cup of hot coffee. Too soon, other people start straggling out of the tents, and the business of the day commences.

After everyone has had breakfast, it's time to change into trail clothes, take down the tents, and pack up the camp. Fill your water bottles again, and if you have a trail thermos, mix up some cocoa for a midmorning break.

During breakfast, I like to set out my sleeping bag in the sun to air out, and I generally make sure the tent floor (warmed by our body heat all night) doesn't freeze to the snow underneath. Often I'll tip over the tent and point its bottom toward the sun to dry.

It's a good idea to discuss the plan for the day over breakfast. The

Try to air out your sleeping bag in camp while everyone's eating breakfast.

whole group is gathered, everyone is warm by the fire if you've made one, and there's time to talk. After breakfast, it's time to pack up, load up, and check out.

When you're ready to go, look thoroughly around camp to see that nothing is left behind and to be sure that the camp area is clean. Finally, when everyone is packed and ready, put out the fire and hit the trail.

Winterlude: America's Snowiest Cities

Among the major American cities, Buffalo, New York, holds the single-season record for the most snowfall. During the winter of 1976–77, 199 inches of the white stuff fell on the city.

Syracuse, New York, has the highest average annual snowfall of all major American cities, averaging 115.6 inches per year. Buffalo, New York, is second with 93.6 inches per year, while Rochester, New York, makes it a trifecta by coming in third with an average of 92.3 inches of snow annually.

U.S. Annual Mean Total Snowfall

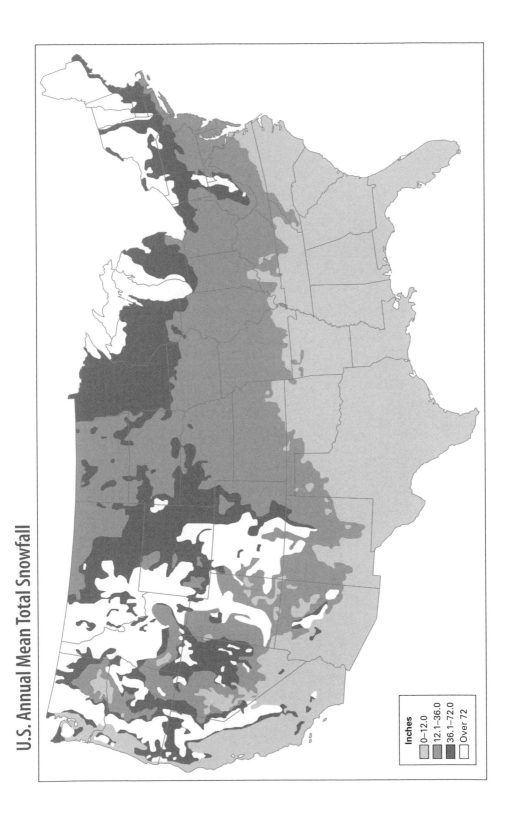

Inches
0–12.0
12.1–36.0
36.1–72.0
Over 72

Chapter 13

Camping with Kids

The scene is a familiar one in the Far North. A snowmobile with two adult passengers pulls a *komatic,* or sled, filled with supplies and camping gear. Nestled in among the supplies, well wrapped against the cold, are the children. An Eskimo family is on the move, heading out to the trap line for a week, 10 days, perhaps a month, perhaps longer.

Winter camping with kids? Why not? For the Eskimo family, there's nothing revolutionary in the idea. For them, taking the children along on the winter trail is nothing more than working a family business. The

An Eskimo girl from Nunavut accompanies her family on the wilderness trail at all times of year.

wilderness is workplace and home, winter and summer, and travel is a part of everyday life. It's unthinkable that the children should not accompany their parents.

The concept of winter living, of being at home in the wild, is an important one for families. It's possible—in fact, it's still common—to travel as a family and care for children in the winter outdoors. What is not possible, however, is making lightweight, high-speed, and technically difficult ascents of remote mountain summits when you travel as a family, at least until the kids are older.

Why camp with kids? If you have kids and you don't camp with them, you either have to leave them with a babysitter or willing relatives, or you have to give up winter camping until they're grown. There are also positive reasons to winter camp with kids: Most kids who spend time outdoors from an early age develop a lifelong appreciation for the natural world. From the time they're very young, they achieve a sense of peaceful well-being and centeredness in nature that many urban people never feel. A connection to the earth—a sense of belonging—is of untold value in the frenetic and ever-changing world we've inherited and will pass on.

We now know that kids who don't spend a lot of time outdoors suffer from Nature Deficit Disorder, a condition with disastrous consequences not only for their physical fitness, but also for their long-term mental and spiritual health.

Over the last few decades, children of the digital age have become increasingly alienated from the natural world. A growing body of scientific research suggests that children who are exposed to nature early and often thrive in intellectual, spiritual, and physical ways that their computer game–playing, instant-messaging peers do not.

The facts speak for themselves, and the news is not good: Two in 10 children are clinically obese—four times the number who were obese in the late 1960s. The number of children diagnosed with Attention Deficit Hyperactivity Disorder (ADHD) shot up by 33 percent from 1997 to 2002. Prescriptions of stimulant medications such as methylphenidate (Ritalin) and amphetamines (Dexedrine) have also skyrocketed, even for preschoolers. Alarmingly, from 2000 to 2003, spending on ADHD drugs for children under the age of five rose 369 percent.

Taking kids into the outdoors is essential if we are to reverse these trends. A 2003 study by researchers at the New York State College of

Human Ecology concluded that exposure to nature resulted in profound increases in children's attention capacities and that "green spaces may enable children to think more clearly and cope more effectively with life stress." The study also found that exposure to nature potentially decreases the symptoms of ADHD.

Another reason to take kids along on winter camping trips is the sense of importance they feel in contributing to the goals of the trip. As with other groups, the success of the family trip depends upon the ability of each member to play a part. No one person or one family member can do everything, but as a family they can do it all—together.

In mainstream society, children, especially teenagers, depend upon adults for everything they need. Tyrannical adults rule the world, set all the conditions, and do everything their own way, and kids suffer from the misery of unimportance. In our complex, modern world it's hard for kids to earn some self-respect, to do something meaningful, to help others, to learn useful skills, to develop a sense of confidence. Mostly, kids are kept in a suffocating position of dependency that can breed frustration.

On a winter camping trip there are plenty of important tasks to perform and many critical skills to master, and this instills self-respect and a sense of competence in young people. Depending upon their age, kids can help erect tents, build snow shelters, collect firewood, carry daypacks, or help with the cooking. Family journeys can work to restore the sense of family purpose and unity that existed before life became so complicated.

Before You Go

Before you put Junior in his snowsuit and herd your family out the door, let's acknowledge that camping, winter or summer, isn't for everyone—and there are no compelling reasons why families must camp together.

Parents may need a hard-earned vacation from their kids and want to go off by themselves. Kids may look forward to spending the week at Grandma's, being spoiled rotten and getting a break from Mom and Dad. Also, even if you love camping, your spouse and your children may not. Family unity isn't strengthened when unwilling or reluctant members are forced to participate in an activity they dislike. Yet if there's support for the idea and if all want to, there are no reasons why families can't go winter camping.

When to Start?

The Eskimo way of life takes children into the wild immediately. A healthy child is remarkably tough and adaptable, and if the child is kept warm and dry (just as you would keep yourself warm and dry), there's no reason why a healthy infant can't go with you. The little lumps are easy enough to take care of, and infants don't complain. As long as they get what they need, they're happy enough to set up shop anywhere. A suite at the Plaza, a tent in the Freeze-Out Range—it's all the same to them. Infants aren't easily impressed. I've seen a number of teeny infants snuggled up in a chest harness, snoozing peacefully as Dad skied along, unencumbered by the tiny weight, breaking trail for the rest of the gang.

To make it easier to get started with winter camping, some families with young children like to team up with other compatible families with young children. Doing so provides adults with friends for support and the children with companions their own age. If you choose to do this, remember not to shortcut the planning process as outlined in chapter 2. Just having young children in common doesn't guarantee that your family's and other family's goals for the trip will be the same. Some families may want to push ahead and cover lots of ground, while other families may want to set up a base camp and explore a smaller area. Families, like individuals, must arrive at an acceptable plan before they take to the woods.

Bring Home with You

Some nervous parents are reluctant to take their kids winter camping because they're afraid they won't be able to care for the children as well in the outdoors as they do at home. Of course they can! The way to do it, of course, is to take home with you and set up shop in a new location. Here again, we're not talking about lightweight, go-fast, do-the-impossible expeditions; we're talking about winter living.

The first step to taking home with you is to view the outdoors as a place where you and your family belong. This takes familiarity, awareness, and a willingness to see yourself as part of nature.

If you can envision yourself and your family being comfortable together in the outdoors, be sure you have your winter skills down before you bring your family with you. You should be adept at everything covered in this book: You should be able to navigate, travel, deal with emergencies, and set up camp with skill and ease. Further, you must be reasonably able to handle any situation in any kind of weather. Your children will be looking to you for guidance, instruction, and support.

Finally, when you have your skills down and feel confident in your abilities, bring home with you. The way to do this is to forget about backpacking and use a sled. It's really the only way to travel on a family trip.

Why Sleds?

You can't possibly transport on your back everything you need in winter plus a child. This is why you need a sled.

A sturdy sled with a rigid harness system is the answer to the needs of winter-camping families, much like a canoe is the answer to summer-camping families. Not only can the kids ride on the sled in warmth, safety, and comfort, but you can carry at least twice and up to three times as much weight on a sled as you can in a pack.

Look at it this way: An absolutely enormous backpack has a volume of around 7,500 cubic inches. A large, commercially available camping sled has a capacity of around 18,000 cubic inches—plenty of room for two kids and gear. If there's still more gear to carry (and you can bring everything you need—diapers, toys, you name it), another adult can carry a pack, or you can load the overflow in a smaller sled (with a volume of about 12,000 cubic inches) that's available to anyone in the group.

Patrick Smith, founder of the Mountainsmith equipment company, designed winter camping sleds so he could take his two young daughters with him on expeditions in the Colorado Rockies. He recommends bundling the children up in their regular winter outfits, putting them on the sled, and "piling in a whole bunch of blankets. If the weather is cold enough, we put them in their sleeping bags too. That's real cozy."

Patrick continues: "Behind the rear seat go the diapers, water, lunch, and so forth. If it's an overnight trip, camping supplies will go with the kids. If there's too much gear, Sarah Jane will have to pack the rest of it or, if there's quite a bit left, she'll put it in the smaller sled. . . . We tend to be pretty lavish with the toys and such."

When the kids are older, bring along their skis or snowshoes and pack these in the sled too. With the sled, they'll always have the option to walk, ski, or ride, and they won't slow you down or wear you out when they get tired.

Sleds are also safer. With a rigid harness, you eliminate front-to-back and side-to-side slipping, and they're very resistant to tipping. If the sled has aluminum runners, it'll track straight behind you and won't slip on a sidling trail. Also, once you get to camp, sleds are efficient at hauling firewood, and if need be, sleds are the method of choice for evacuating a sick or injured camper.

A well-made sled with all the options is not cheap, but it will cost less than two large-volume backpacks. Plus, as Patrick says, "I look at it this way: Figure out how much it costs to pay for a babysitter for a day out on the trail. It's that simple. Many folks will pay for their sled in one season in babysitter savings alone. But the bottom line still has to be that your little one(s) will be with you, sharing the outdoors with you and having a great, and safe, time to boot."

Special Considerations

Camping with kids isn't all that complicated, and most fears of overprotective parents are either exaggerated or groundless. Kids won't break, and kids are people too. They're tough, and their needs aren't all that different from your own, so everything that goes for adults goes for kids as well. Kids need to drink a lot, eat well, wear layers, use sunglasses or goggles, and generally do whatever their parents are doing.

Yet kids may not be able to tell you that they're too hot, too cold, thirsty, hungry, or exhausted, so parents need to be extra vigilant to recognize their children's needs. When kids accompany adults, the parents are the leaders and must accept the additional burden of responsibility that goes with that role. This is all the more reason for parents to have solid winter camping and leadership skills before they take their children with them.

Here are some points to consider when you're thinking of taking kids with you.

Planning. Be flexible. Go through the planning process as outlined in chapter 2, but build in more options. Recognize that you won't be able to cover as much ground every day as you might if you're traveling only with adults. Even if you pull your children in a sled, don't make every day a forced march. With kids, while 4 or 5 miles a day may be fun, 6 or 7 might be a drag. Forget about the odometer; red-line the fun meter and be willing and able to change your plans if necessary. Also, if you keep travel time to a minimum and set up a base camp, you'll have more flexibility in deciding how to spend the day.

Make it fun. Plan on making the experience fun for your kids. Try to look at the trip from their point of view. Imagine what a good time the kids will have building snow caves, sledding, and skiing! The winter outdoors puts any playground or amusement park to shame. Think how entrancing a campfire will be, how mysterious the sound of a coyote howling.

Make it fun on the way in, too. Remember that long, uphill climbs may not be as much fun as easier terrain with lots of exciting downhills. What's more, constant instruction from adults can quickly turn a fun outing into an ordeal, so allow kids to learn through self-discovery, experience, and by watching what you do. Instead of formal instruction in skiing and snowshoeing, for example, games such as tag and follow the leader will have them flashing around in no time.

Make it informative. The fastest way to turn kids off to the outdoors is to provide them with second-hand, encyclopedic knowledge about plants, animals, and other features of the natural environment. Memorized information gleaned from textbooks or field guides can be stagnant and sterile, and it conveys little sense of the intricate relationships in nature.

Children are incredibly perceptive and imaginative. They're far more likely to understand how nature works by experiencing it than they are by learning dry facts. For example, to a child a raven is a magical black bird with a most remarkable croaking voice that takes great pleasure in tumbling on the wind, scavenging animal remains, and watching all camp activities with an intense curiosity. The experience of being with this bird in a wild setting may pique their interest and spur them to learn more about it.

Let your children do the exploring. Answer their questions if they have any, but don't close the doors for them. Instead, let them rekindle your own sense of wonder; let them help you rediscover your own ability to understand complex relationships with childlike enthusiasm.

Rest. Build in plenty of time for rest, especially on a travel day. Even if the kids don't need a rest, they may need a chance to run around, poke about, or toss snowballs. Give them a handful of gorp and let them play. Join in if you're up to it. Re-evaluate your plan for the day at rest stops. If the kids are too tired, unhappy, or otherwise put out, decide whether it makes sense to continue or to stop and set up camp early. Constantly monitor the situation as it develops.

Clothing. Children essentially wear what their parents wear. Many outdoor-clothing manufacturers make a full line of kid's winter clothing—

from long underwear to balaclavas—so you can layer your kids the same way you layer yourselves. If they're infants, be sure to bring several changes.

Safety. You can teach children about safety in the winter environment the same way you teach them about safety at home, where there are many more dangers—stoves, lawnmowers, automobile traffic, hazardous liquids—for them to blunder into than there are outdoors. When they understand about hot woodstoves (as they understand about hot stoves at home), splitting wood with a sharp ax, windchill, and snow and ice characteristics, they'll treat these with respect.

Teach them what you know about stream crossings, for instance, the same way you teach them how to cross a street—by looking carefully before you go. Tell them what to look for. Crossing ice will be just like crossing the street for them, a part of their everyday environment—something they can do safely, intelligently, and without undue concern.

Outdoor tools and activities somehow seem more dangerous than home tools and activities because we're less familiar with them. This is not an accurate way to assess risk. By any measure, driving in an automobile is by far the most dangerous activity most of us will ever engage in, yet because it's so familiar to us, we don't give it a second thought. If you familiarize your children with the winter environment and teach them what to look for and what to avoid, they'll be as safe as—or safer than—they are at home.

Experienced winter campers with children will find that taking their kids with them adds new dimensions to their experience, perhaps rekindling their own sense of wonder and excitement as they share the outdoors with their youngsters. As Patrick Smith says, "I can't really say it's easy—more like it's worth it."

Chapter 14

Cold Injuries

Wherever you go at whatever time of year, there are environmental hazards. Beachgoers must avoid sunburn. Suburban gardeners keep an eye out for poison ivy and ticks. Every place has its dangers, but when they're known and precautions are taken, they can be avoided.

The outdoors in winter has its own perils for the unprepared. Compounding the problem, these situations can be brought on or aggravated by the existence of the more common stresses facing a wilderness traveler: fatigue, dehydration, and the usual assorted knocks, scrapes and bruises. The winter camper must exhibit an especially high level of awareness and vigilance when it comes to dealing with environmental hazards. The most important and common winter camping hazards are hypothermia (the condition of having a lower-than-normal body temperature) and frostbite (the freezing of body tissues). These are medical emergencies occurring when the body is stressed to an excessive degree by the effects of cold weather. Another fairly common winter injury is snowblindness (the condition of having sunburned the eyes). Snowblindness happens when the eyes absorb high levels of ultraviolet radiation.

All of these conditions are preventable, yet every winter camper should be familiar with the symptoms and treatment of these cold-weather injuries.

Hypothermia

Hypothermia occurs when the body loses heat faster than it can be generated. If the loss isn't arrested and the situation brought under control, hypothermia can be fatal.

Body heat is produced through eating, drinking warm fluids, and exercise such as walking, running, or even shivering. It can also be acquired from an external source such as the sun, a fire, or another warm body. Body heat is best maintained by carefully monitoring and controlling it like a precious currency; don't spend it all in one place at one time.

Not all body heat loss is a bad. Remember the layering principle: Layering allows excess heat to escape so you avoid a perspiration drenching. Uncontrolled heat loss is the enemy to be guarded against. The body loses heat in any of four ways.

- **Radiation.** A significant amount of body heat can be lost when it's emitted directly into the environment because of a lack of insulation. An uncovered head, for example, radiates an enormous amount of heat that's immediately dissipated and lost.
- **Conduction.** Heat can be lost through conduction when you come into direct physical contact with something cold, whether it's the cold ground, frigid water, or clothing saturated with sweat, rain, or melted snow.
- **Convection.** Your body generates enough heat to keep warm the layer of air directly next to the skin. Your clothing maintains this warm layer by trapping it in the dead air spaces of the fabric. That layer of warm air can quickly be stolen by the wind—through convection—if you don't wear proper shell garments.
- **Evaporation.** When you breathe, you inhale cold air, which is warmed to body temperature, saturated with moisture, and then exhaled. This continual replacement of warm, moist air by cold, dry air causes evaporative heat loss. Perspiration also contributes to heat loss because the body must generate considerable heat in order to turn the moisture to vapor and disperse it through evaporation.

Uncontrolled heat loss through any of these mechanisms or a combination of them can lead to a situation in which the amount of heat lost is greater than the amount your body produces. The result: hypothermia. Cold, wet, windy days are the times to be especially wary.

Stages of Hypothermia

Humans are truly equatorial animals. We need to maintain a constant body temperature of 98.6 degrees or we become quite uncomfortable. Even a drop of a few degrees impairs our ability to function normally or even survive—and a few degrees' drop results in the early stages of hypothermia. A few more degrees results in deeper hypothermia. Here's what to look for in cases of hypothermia.

- **Early stages.** The early stages of hypothermia (body temperature of

98.6 to about 95.0) are characterized by fits of intense shivering and an inability to control muscular coordination. The victim feels cold, tired, and confused.

- **Middle stages.** As hypothermia progresses (body temperature of 95.0 to 90.0) the victim continues to shiver violently—the body's way of trying to generate enough warmth to make up for the loss which is occurring. The victim experiences difficulty in speaking, thinking, and walking. His judgment is impaired, and he may suffer from amnesia and hallucinations. Apathy, even lack of awareness concerning his situation, sets in.
- **Late middle stages.** By now (body temperature of 90.0 to 86.0) the victim has stopped shivering and has lost the ability to rewarm himself. He can no longer walk or speak. His muscles are rigid, his skin turns blue (cyanotic), and his pulse and respiration slow perceptibly. He passes into a state of stupor.
- **Late stages.** As the victim continues to cool (body temperature of 86.0 to 78.0), he becomes unconscious. He is nonresponsive and his pulse and respiration may not be noticeable. A body temperature that falls below 78.0 degrees results in death, usually from a combination of heart and respiratory failure.

Early Detection and Avoidance of Hypothermia

The way to avoid hypothermia is, of course, through awareness and prevention. Put on proper clothing before you get wet, and take it off before you overheat and perspire.

Protect yourself from the cooling effects of wind, water, and cold surfaces. Be prepared to turn back from your objective or wait out a storm if necessary. Don't be afraid to change your plan if a dangerous situation arises. Conserve your energy, eat and drink well, and don't push too hard.

Watch for the telltale signs of hypothermia in others; some of us call them the "umbles": stumbles, mumbles, fumbles, grumbles. Anyone exhibiting these behaviors is probably not well. It's best to stop and deal with the situation before it progresses.

Treatment of Hypothermia

As soon as it becomes apparent that a member of the party is hypothermic, stop and check the rest of the group; if one person is exhibiting the symptoms, chances are high that others may be in the same condition. Stop traveling and set up camp immediately.

As with ice and avalanche rescue, these procedures must be rehearsed in advance of an actual emergency. Everyone must react quickly and efficiently. Set up the tents, build a fire, light the stoves, and heat the water. Meanwhile, someone must remain with the victim at all times and take charge of the overall situation.

Those in the early stages of hypothermia must have warmth, food, and fluids immediately. Get the victim out of wet clothes and into dry ones. Place him near a source of heat, such as a fire or another person. Putting the victim in a sleeping bag with another person works well as a rewarming strategy, but only if the nonhypothermic person is wearing light layers of dry clothing. If the rescuer is naked, his or her sweat will continue to chill the victim and may actually prolong the crisis.

If the victim is in the middle to later stages of hypothermia and is no longer able to rewarm himself, the rescuers must take even more active measures. The victim must be handled very gently in a controlled, protected environment, such as a tent. External sources of heat must be provided, and all possible heat loss must be stopped.

First, insulate the victim from the cold ground with sleeping pads, extra clothing, pine boughs, or whatever else is on hand. Place at the victim's neck, groin, and underarms chemical heat packs or water bottles filled with warm water (not too hot to the touch). You can wrap the heat packs or water bottles in extra layers of long underwear or stuff sacks to keep them from burning or overheating the victim.

Place the victim in a prewarmed sleeping bag. Next, wrap him in a tarp, tent fly, or reflective blanket—whatever waterproof and windproof fabric is available—to cut heat loss through radiation and convection. If the victim is conscious, allow him to sip very sweet liquids, such as extra thick cocoa, liquid Jell-O, or some other supersweet instant beverage mix. The sugar will help replace energy reserves depleted by long bouts of shivering. Do not force liquids on an unconscious person.

If the victim lapses into unconsciousness or is lacking in all apparent vital activity, continue treatment and prepare for evacuation. Use extreme gentleness if you need to move him at all. Although this functioning may be undetectable, the heart may be operating at a very low level and any rough handling of the victim may cause it to cease altogether. There have been cases of apparently lifeless hypothermic individuals being successfully resuscitated with no lasting ill effects.

Frostbite

I was climbing Mount Adams in New Hampshire's Presidential Range on a stunning midwinter day. The sky was a sharp blue, the slopes were a crisp white, and a brilliant sun shone high overhead. With an air temperature of –20 degrees, however, and a steady wind blowing at 50 to 60 miles per hour with gusts even higher, the windchill effect was around –85 degrees.

On a day like this, wind protection is essential, and every inch of my skin was covered—well, almost. As I turned into the wind to begin the descent, I felt a searing pain, just like the sting of a wasp, on my cheek. I turned out of the wind to readjust my face mask and goggles. Too late. A blister the size of my thumbnail was already raised on my cheek where a sliver of skin had been exposed for only a few seconds—plenty of time for the skin to flash-freeze in such conditions.

Frostbite is the freezing of body tissues and may result in little or no damage to the affected area if it's dealt with early on. Yet if the case is severe and worsens, frostbite may result in permanent damage or even loss of the affected body parts. Like hypothermia, the condition is completely preventable if winter travelers are aware and take the proper precautions.

Symptoms of frostbite can include pallor of the skin caused by a lack of blood reaching the affected area, a sensation of numbness or pain as the tissues begin to freeze, and blistering, as occurred in my case. If the frostbite is allowed to progress unchecked, the skin turns white and hard, and eventually the affected area becomes frozen solid.

Insulating the body against the mechanisms of heat loss—radiation, convection, conduction, and evaporation—easily prevents frostbite. Active prevention of hypothermia will go a long way toward the prevention of frostbite.

When frostbite is still in the early stages, the affected area can usually be rewarmed by direct contact with another person's warm skin, such as putting a camper's cold feet against another camper's belly, tucking frostbitten fingers under armpits, or holding a frostbitten cheek in a warm hand.

If the frostbite is more severe and medical help isn't available, rapid rewarming in warm water is the best treatment. Immerse the frostbitten body part in water warmed to approximately 105 degrees. Before immersion, test the temperature of the water with a thermometer. If you don't have one, test the water by dipping your elbow into it. The water should feel pleasantly warm, like a hot bath, but not too hot to the touch. Keep the frostbitten part immersed until it has been thoroughly thawed.

Before making the decision to rewarm a body part in the field, be aware that if the affected area is refrozen, it's very likely to result in even greater damage, so if the conditions that caused the initial freezing persist—inadequate clothing, an inability to protect the frostbitten part—then field rewarming is not a good idea.

Keep in mind also that if the feet are affected, thawing will incapacitate the victim, making it necessary for the rest of the group to carry him out. Walking on frozen feet, however, will most likely result in little or no additional damage to the tissues.

Finally, rewarming a deeply frozen area is excruciatingly painful, so it may be best to keep the affected area in a stable condition until you obtain medical help.

Snowblindness

March in Colorado can be a backcountry skier's paradise. With a foot of new powder and plenty of sunshine, our day was as good as it gets. All day we floated down sunny slopes until we finally returned to camp, exhausted but happy, anxious to start all over the next day.

Around midnight, however, I woke up feeling as though someone was driving thumbtacks into my eyes. The pain was almost unimaginable. Cold compresses helped, but the agony persisted.

Hours later, when pain medications were applied and my eyes were bandaged, the pain finally abated. Becoming snow blind is a memorable experience, but one I hope never to repeat.

Snowblindness is sunburn of the eyes. As with other forms of sunburn (a surprisingly common winter affliction), snowblindness occurs when your eyes are not adequately protected from the harmful rays of the sun reflecting off the surface of the snow.

Prevention of Snowblindness

Snowblindness is completely preventable by wearing dark sunglasses or goggles with high-quality lenses. Sometimes, as in the mountains of the western United States and Canada or in the Arctic, it's most often suggested that you wear mountaineering glasses with side flaps to prevent excess light from entering.

If you lose your sunglasses and goggles, try to make a pair of Eskimo goggles: Give a piece of birch bark, cardboard, or wood the shape of a pair of goggles and cut lengthwise slits in it to see through. Rub charcoal over the inside of these slits to further reduce the glare assaulting your eyes. Finally, tie the makeshift goggles around your head with string.

Treatment of Snowblindness

Victims of snowblindness will recover in two or three days. In the meantime, if medical help isn't available, cold compresses, painkillers, and darkness will help. Plan on making camp for a couple of days until the victim is prepared to travel again.

Evacuation

Sometimes victims of hypothermia, frostbite, or other injuries suffered in the field need medical attention as soon as possible. After the group has done everything it can to treat the victim and the situation remains critical, the members must decide whether or not to try to evacuate the injured traveler or seek outside help.

If the injuries are severe, the group size is small, and the terrain is complex, the party may deem it wise to send for outside help. In such a situation the group must realize that aid may be a long time in arriving. Some group members may wish to begin evacuation while others go for assistance. At other times, if the victim can't be moved—if he has a neck injury, for example—make him as comfortable as possible, monitor his condition, and await the return of the rescue party.

Sending for Help

Two people should go for help. They must travel as swiftly as possible in a safe manner. Safety is paramount over speed—the victim and the ones remaining behind have placed all of their hopes for assistance in the hands of the messengers. They must arrive safely to deliver the summons.

The messengers should be provided with adequate food, clothing, and equipment, but should not be weighed down by extraneous items. They

Snow School

How big were the largest snowflakes ever measured?

Snowflakes that were 15 inches in diameter were recorded on January 28, 1887, near Fort Keogh, Montana. •

must bring a map precisely identifying the location of the victim, and they must be able to retrace their route. Flagging the route with duct tape can expedite the return journey if necessary.

Finally, the messengers must clearly articulate the nature of the problem to the appropriate authorities and make sure that the rescue is set in motion.

Self-Rescue by the Group

If the group can handle the evacuation by themselves, so much the better. Sending for help necessarily means exposing more people to potentially dangerous situations. If that can be avoided, everyone benefits.

When the terrain is not complex and the rescue is not technically difficult, the group may be better off initiating the rescue themselves rather than waiting for outside help. If the group has been traveling with sleds or toboggans, they're probably already in good shape to proceed.

All that remains is to bundle the victim as described in the section on hypothermia (page 199) and secure him to the sled. Two or three people can then pull the sled with ropes attached to the front. For the most efficient pulling, tie loops in the ropes to go across one shoulder and under the opposite arm. The ropes should be of different lengths so the people pulling can march in single file and still take turns breaking trail.

A rope should be attached to the rear of the sled to control it on the downhills. Trees can be used to belay the sled down steep slopes in a controlled fashion.

If the victim's injuries are not debilitating but still deserve medical attention, wait until he's ready to proceed with evacuation. A period of rest will do no harm and may refresh the victim enough to make the trip with only basic assistance.

Winter campers are also subject to the more common afflictions associated with outdoor living, such as sunburn, gastrointestinal problems, and other minor complaints. Before you head out the door, take a solid, basic first aid course and review books on backcountry medicine.

Afterword

As winter enthusiasts, we're especially concerned about the threat of climate change. A warming world is not friendly to backcountry skiing and riding. Yet pointing fingers at others while counting carbon parts per billion without making personal lifestyle changes is not enough. There's a lot of talk about global warming, but not a lot of action being taken on the

The Vermont winter woods at sunset are worth preserving for future generations of winter campers and outdoor travelers.

individual level. If we want to keep enjoying pristine winter environments, we all need to embrace the old-fashioned principles of conservation: Reduce. Reuse. Recycle. Restore.

Now more than ever we must recognize that, as E. F. Schumacher said, "The real problems facing all living things on this planet are not economic or technical, they are philosophical."

Despite our blind faith in our amazing ability to tinker, there are no magic technical bullets to preserve the environment. No green technology will keep winter cold, wild, and white. Only changed human behavior will do that.

As Henry David Thoreau said, "In wildness is the preservation of the world."

Other Places to Learn

I n addition to learning from this book, learning from more experienced
winter travelers will help you to develop skills at your own pace in a
safe environment. Build a solid base of knowledge that you can add to as
you gain experience and expand your comfort zone. Following are de-
scriptions of some of the best ways to get started in winter camping.

Outdoors-Skills Schools

There are several outdoor-skills schools operating in the United States and
Canada, and some of them offer excellent instruction in winter camping.
Before you sign up for a course, find out as much as you can about the
school: its educational philosophy, the qualifications of the instructional
staff, the age and background of the typical student, and the curriculum.
Remember that most outdoor schools are tailored to meet the needs of
high school and college students, although many are now offering courses
for older students, women, and other groups.

The best outdoor-skills schools have highly trained, personable instructors and offer a variety of courses. Try to gain a clear understanding
of the curriculum and determine if it meets your needs. Read the literature, talk to course graduates, and make an informed decision.

Guided Trips

Until about the middle of the 19th century, it was almost unthinkable for
even experienced people to head off into the wilderness without a native
guide. There was good reason for this practice: The guide was usually a
local resident who made his living in the woods and led guests on the side.

Some guide services in the far north offer dogsled expeditions, such as this one on Hudson Bay

In an era before precise mapping, it was important to travel with someone who knew the land.

Improved mapping systems and easier access have made the wilderness less remote, and while the idea of hiring a guide might seem out of date, there still may be no better way to learn skills than from a good guide. Most guides offer a broad selection of services, ranging from outfitting equipment and providing transportation to leading trips. Some guide services have a schedule of arranged trips you can join, but they may also work with you to design a custom trip. The level of involvement is up to you. Typically, the more you're involved in the planning and organizing of the trip, the more you'll learn.

Guide services are everywhere, from the Canadian Arctic to the Maine woods. There are services that offer dogsled expeditions, ski tours, mountaineering trips, and even journeys to the Poles.

As with outdoor schools, learn as much as you can before you sign up for a trip. This may be more difficult because some of the best services are very small with word-of-mouth reputations. Ask for personal references; ask about the guides' training and about their backgrounds and qualifications.

Outing Clubs

There are outing clubs in most parts of North America, particularly in areas near the mountains. These clubs often have an education or excursion department that sponsors workshops and skills-training courses. Some of these organizations are quite large and have national reputations; others are local volunteer groups. Regardless, clubs are an excellent way to get started in winter camping. The people usually represent a broad spectrum of ages, abilities, backgrounds, and interests; the instructors are often well-qualified and highly competent members; and the costs can be significantly less than those of an outdoor-school course or guided trip. An added bonus to a club outing is getting to know the other members and planning future trips together.

Stores and Specialty Shops

Outdoor stores often organize trips and skills workshops for their customers and other interested parties. Local residents attend these trips, usually to a local or regional destination. This is a great way to discover the special attributes of your area and to get to know potential partners for future trips.

Books

Books such as this one can teach you a lot about winter camping. Learning from a how-to book is a three-part process: study, practice, and study some more. Every time you return to a chapter after having tried what it suggests, you'll better understand the information.

First Aid Kit

No first aid kit has everything you need to handle every possible medical scenario in the outdoors, but the following list, combined with basic first aid knowledge, is adequate for most common backcountry afflictions.

Ace bandage

Acetaminophen tablets

Adhesive tape

Alcohol swabs

Antacid tablets

Antihistamine tablets

Antiseptic solution

Antiseptic ointment

Aspirin tablets

Band-Aids

Butterfly Band-Aids or steri-strips

Chemical heat packs

Gauze pads (4 inches by 4 inches)

Hydrocortisone ointment

Ibuprofen tablets

Moleskin

Personal medications

Roll of gauze bandaging

Safety pins

Sanitary napkins

Scissors

Sunscreen

Tweezers

Triangular bandage

If you're heading into a remote area where medical help is several days away, consult your doctor when putting together your first aid kit.

The Hut-to-Hut Alternative

Backcountry hut and yurt skiing means staying inside a toasty cabin instead of curling up in a tent or snow cave. There's something truly wonderful and restorative about spending time in the winter wilds in a remote cabin. Even experienced winter campers enjoy the luxury of staying in these secluded wilderness hideaways from time to time.

As with winter camping, however, wilderness hut touring also means venturing into the wild on your own, perhaps beyond assistance. Have fun, but ski or snowboard cautiously. Bring the proper food, clothing, equipment, and knowledge, and have a plan for dealing with emergencies.

There are excellent hut-to-hut and yurt systems throughout North America. Here are some of the best.

Alaska

Resurrection Pass Cabins

If you're ready to sample a real Alaskan adventure but aren't quite prepared to watch as your last connection to civilization tips its wings and vanishes over the horizon, you may be ready for the Resurrection Pass Trail. The eight rustic cabins along the trail provide welcome shelter from wintry weather. Maintained and rented out by the U.S. Forest Service, the cabins are quite cozy but very simple, providing only bunks, a table and benches, and a woodstove, so you bring the rest. For more information, visit www.reserveusa.com.

California

Sierra Club Huts

The Sierra Club operates five huts in the Lake Tahoe area near some of the best backcountry skiing in North America. The huts are a day's ski apart from each other or about a day's travel from various trailheads, so experienced, well-equipped groups may undertake multiday tours along the crest of the Sierras without needing to camp. For the less adventurous, the huts can still be accessed for overnight or weekend stays. The huts feature woodstoves and bunks, but visitors must bring sleeping bags, utensils, candles, and other personal equipment. For more information, visit www.sierraclub.org.

Colorado

10th Mountain Division Hut System

The most extensive hut system in North America and the standard by which others are measured, the 10th Mountain Division System consists of 29 huts scattered throughout the heart of the Rockies between Aspen, Vail, and Leadville. The huts make possible extended wilderness tours in

The Harry Gates hut in the 10th Mountain Division Hut System

spectacular high mountain settings. The huts are fully equipped with photovoltaic electricity, woodstoves and propane burners, cookware, and bunks. Bring your own food and sleeping bag. For more information, visit www.huts.org.

Quebec
Chic-Choc Huts

This hut system may have more to offer the winter adventurer than any of the others combined. The Chic-Choc Mountains jut sharply from the vast Parc national de la Gaspesie of the Gaspé Peninsula in Quebec. The backcountry terrain of the park is wild, steep, and very, very snowy. Moreover, it boasts one of the continent's largest networks of huts, rivaling Colorado's extensive 10th Mountain Division Hut System. In the Chic-Chocs it's possible to winter camp, ski hut-to-hut, spend a night at a comfortable lodge in the heart of the mountains, or do all three. Highly accessible to the northeastern United States, the Chic-Chocs offer an extremely alpine, subarctic adventure. This is the only place in North America where you may see white-tailed deer, moose, and caribou on the same day. Add to this its rich trove of French history and its foreign-culture cachet, and you have all the elements for a truly wonderful hut-to-hut experience. For more information, visit www.sepaq.org.

Minnesota
Gunflint Trail Lodges

Miles of wilderness ski trails wind through northern Minnesota's Boundary Waters area. There are few hair-raising downhill runs here in the north woods, but there's plenty of cross-country touring through deep wilderness solitude. For a variation on the hut-to-hut theme, try a cross-country trek with overnight stops in Mongolian yurts. Each yurt features a woodstove, fully equipped kitchen, sleeping bags, and bunk beds. For more information, visit www.boundarycountry.com.

Index

W

water, drinking, 118, 174–76
wax kits, 74–75
weather forecasts, 43–44
whistles, 77
Whorf, Benjamin Lee, 45
wildlife, 132–35